THE CHRISTIAN MIND

Also by Dom Anscar Vonier
Published by Assumption Press

The Human Soul and its Relations with Other Spirits

The Personality of Christ

A Key to the Doctrine of the Eucharist

The Divine Motherhood

The Life of the World to Come

The Art of Christ: Retreat Conferences

The Angels

Death and Judgement

The New and Eternal Covenant

Christ the King of Glory

Christianus

The Victory of Christ

The Spirit and the Bride

The People of God

Sketches and Studies in Theology

The Christian Mind

Dom Anscar Vonier

Abbot of Buckfast

2014

✠ Nihil Obstat.
F. Thos. Bergh,
Censor Deputatus.

✠ Imprimatur.
Edm. Can. Surmont,
Vicarius Generalis.

Westminster
May 12, 1918.

The *Nihil Obstat* and *Imprimatur* are official declarations that a book or pamphlet is free of doctrinal or moral error. No implication is contained therein that those who have granted the *Nihil Obstat* and the *Imprimatur* agree with the content, opinions or statements expressed.

Copyright © 2014 Assumption Press. This material may not be reproduced, displayed, modified or distributed without the express prior written permission of the copyright holder.

This book was originally published in 1920 by B. Herder.

Cover image: *St. Paul Writing his Epistles*, Valentin de Boulogne, c. 1618-20

Contents

Foreword...i

1. Christian Theology and the Christian Mind.....1
2. Two Views of the Son of God 6
3. The Role of Christ's Humanity..............12
4. The Necessity of Possessing the Christian Mind . 16
5. Special Christian Mind Versus General Christian Mind....................21
6. A Short Criticism of the Mental Attitude of Christians......................25
7. St. Paul's Mind........................30
8. St. Paul's Argumentations..................34
9. The New Creature in Christ................54
10. The Central Attitude of the Christian Mind ... 61
11. Our Equality in Christ...................68
12. The Christian Mind and Eternal Life 73
13. The Christian Mind and Death.............81
14. The Attitude of the Christian Mind Towards them that Fall Asleep in the Lord .. 88
15. Christ the Judge of the Living and the Dead ... 96
16. Putting on Christ 106
17. The Christian Mind, The Church, and the Eucharist..................121

Conclusion 131

Foreword

It is the experience of every observer how reluctant Christian men and women are to embrace bravely and ungrudgingly with their mind the practical conclusions that flow from the great mystery of the Incarnation. Ever so many Christians, even amongst those who profess piety, and possess education, shape their thoughts, and order their lives, on principles that have no direct relationship with the central fact of Christianity, the Incarnate Son of God.

I have tried in the following pages to draw a distinction between general spirituality, and the specific Christian spirituality, which is based on the practical assimilation by our minds of the doctrine of the Incarnation. The purpose of the book is, of course, more of the nature of a philosophy of the Christian religion, than of a hortatory, or preceptive character.

It is a modest contribution to that effort of which there are so many instances in Western Christendom in our days, of building up a Christian mind, as a power of thought that rules in virtue of its own innate truthfulness and excellency.

In the building of a great fane even the one that carries the hod feels that he is doing a great work.

My book might easily be compared with the labors of the carrier of the hod, even by a kind critic, as there is such an accumulation of scriptural texts through these pages. There seems little art required to string together quotations from Holy Writ. I must submit completely to this judgment, with the assurance however that the kind of result I aim at could not be obtained otherwise. To each man his task, be it mean or noble, in rearing up the most glorious of all spiritual buildings, the Christian Mind.

Buckfast Abbey, Easter 1918.
Anscar Vonier, O. S. B., Abbot.

The Christian Mind

I

CHRISTIAN THEOLOGY AND THE CHRISTIAN MIND

*T*he doctrines concerning Christ's sacred Person stand out before the Christian intellect as a clearly defined and full grown body of dogmas. This body of dogmas has reached maturity long ago, and unlike man's bodily frame, it keeps its freshness and health and vigor and youthfulness unimpaired as the world grows older.

The doctrines respecting Christ's Person are commonly designated under the term Christology. It may be said that Christology as a series of doctrines reached its perfection at the end of the eighth century of the Christian era. By that time the universal councils of the Church had made it clear, for all times, what are the true elements that enter into the composition of that wonderful Personality, Jesus Christ.

Later councils, as, for instance, the council of Trent, have defined many doctrines concerning Christ's share in the work of man's salvation, but they did not add anything to our knowledge of the mystery of Christ's Person, considered in Himself. The great Doctors of the Church, and foremost amongst them St. Augustine of Hippo and St. Thomas Aquinas, have made it their task to explain to the thinking Christian intellect the meaning and the far reaching bearing of the great Church definitions in this matter of the God Incarnate. Taken together with the pronouncements of the Church, the explanations furnished by the great divines in their theological treatises form a body of thought of the supremest intellectual order, independently of their value as Christian dogmas.

The doctrines of Christology are truths of the highest order, and no intellect could busy itself with them without reaching a high mental perfection, besides having the merit of the obedience of faith. The God Incarnate, however, is essentially and intrinsically the life of individual souls. It is His most constant and solemn assertion that He is life, man's life.

The life of the Christian therefore has a function that is all its own, namely to express and translate into actuality Christ, the Son of God; for the Son of God could not be man's life, unless man's life had it for one of its organic functions to give expression to the Son of God.

To be the Son of God, and to be the life of man, is the most adequate definition of Our Lord's role. Christology, or the theology of the Incarnation, is primarily concerned with the wondrous fact that Christ is the Son of God. It is chiefly theoretical in nature. As I said a moment ago, it is a marvelous system of doctrines that has reached maturity, and I might say, finality, long ago.

But Christ's other role, that of being the life of man, is still to a great extent an unexplored field of immense spiritual possibilities, at least for individual souls. It is simply impossible to tell to what extent individual souls may find Christ to be their life. The past exhibits some very glorious patterns of Christ as the life of man. The future may have in store other and no less surprising manifestations of the same life.

When I say here that Christ's role as the life of man is an unexplored field of spiritual possibilities, I owe my reader a word of explanation. There are, of course, the clearly defined doctrines of the influence and action of mankind's Redeemer on mankind.

The Church has pronounced on all matters that are pertinent to the general question of man's salvation and sanctification through Christ. Such doctrines are really part of our general Christology: they share its maturity and its finality. But when all doctrines concerning our Lord, both in Himself and in His action on souls, have been enumerated, there still remains another realm of supernatural realities that invites exploration.

The question is this: how does a man behave, to whom the Incarnation and all that it implies has become a living fact, and in whom the Son of God is an actual and pulsating life? How does such a man feel, how does he act, what does he dare, what view does he take of man in life and death? What sort of mind has he, what sort of heart, what sort of character?

And more generally, how far is the Incarnation capable of producing a specific character, a specific mind, in the people who believe it all literally, without any reservations? Is there, or can there be, here on earth, a race of men and women whose characters, whose minds, are not only modified, but are actually created by sincere and living belief in the Son of God, so that a great dramatist could place them in some heroic play, as he could be quite certain of the workings of such characters?

In one word, putting it more learnedly: is there, or can there be, a psychology of the Incarnation in men and women as truly as there is the psychology of nationality and race and heredity and environment, and what are the elements of such a psychology?

Put in this wise, the matter becomes clearly distinguished from the more generic question as to Christ's share in man's redemption. It is distinction between principles and character. The great truths of Catholic Christology are the principles. What we are trying to find out now, is the sort of character such principles are able to produce, and do produce in reality.

Or again it is a distinction between theory and life. To hold the doctrines of the Incarnation in their entirety may still be considered as theory, but to live such theories and such doctrines is evidently quite a different matter. It constitutes a new spiritual phenomenon of endless freshness and variability, of which a man who otherwise admits every one of the articles of the Christian creed may be devoid.

The present book is an analytical study of the specific spiritual character produced in man by the principle of traditional Christology. It is a study of Christian character, as opposed to Christian theology. By "Christian," I mean here the Christ-thing, in its own specific nature. (It is a pity that there is no adjective derived from the word Christ, so as to enable us to express easily and promptly the ideas that contain attributes which are meant for the Son of God in Person. The word "Christian" hardly means Christ in adjective form.)

When I speak of character, psychology, and life as opposed to doctrine, dogma, and theology, the opposition is, of course, not an opposition of contrariety, as character is caused by doctrine, and though it be something distinct, yet it bears the stamp of doctrine.

It has occurred to me that the expression "Christian Mind" would be an appropriate enough title for a book whose object it is to analyze and to describe the kind of psychology bred in man through a practical assimilation of the wondrous truths of the Incarnation. Mind is something between mere Intellect and conduct. It is both a view and a behavior. It is something more than character, as it implies a relish and a keenness for wide views, a thing not necessarily contained in character.

Mind again has a practical side which does not belong to mere intellect, or to speculative thought, and is more intimately part of our individual life than abstract truths, or doctrines held by our faith. So all things considered, I think that my title "The Christian Mind" is not a misnomer for the matter I have to treat. I might have called the book "Christian Psychology", were it not for the circumstance that the term savors too much of a technicality.

The matter of the book brings its own division. On the one hand we may consider the Christian mind from the point of view of a mere possibility, that is to say from the study of the truths of the Incarnation, and we may tell at once what sort of mind could be bred in man if he made such doctrine his own, if he followed them up in life logically and fearlessly. Then we may take a Christian mind from the realm of actuality, a man who has lived Christ thoroughly and boldly, and whose whole mind, thus transformed, has been revealed to his fellow Christians.

We have such a man in the person of St Paul. So a considerable portion of the book amounts really to a character-study of St. Paul. For a long time it had been my intention to call the book "The Christ of St. Paul," but the more general title under which the book goes forth now will enable me to give my studies a scope even wider than the mind of St. Paul. Even St. Paul did not express in his life the totality of Christ.

It is not my intention, however, to divide the book ostensibly into two sections, though its matter be twofold, conjectural and actual. But the book will be a blending both of spiritual possibilities, such as the Incarnation may produce, and of the spiritual actualities, such as it did produce in Paul of Tarsus.

II

Two Views of the Son of God

The Catholic doctrines concerning Christ's Divine Personality, however lofty and speculative they may seem at first sight, are found, sooner or later, to be the sources of living waters for the humblest soul, and to give life and growth to the tiniest spiritual plant.

There is hardly a more impressive spectacle in nature than the sight exhibited in some of the great mountain systems of Europe. A great mountain rises straight up to the sky, its flanks forming a sheer precipice, a rugged wall of rocks; and from the rock there leaps a fully formed stream, born as it were in full manhood, beginning its career with a great volume of water, there being none of that silent oozing out from the ground of Waters that meet gently, and gradually form themselves into a rivulet. No, the dry hard rock itself lets loose a fully formed stream. It is, of course, the overflow of the ever active lakes inside the mountain fastness.

What strikes the observer when he comes upon a phenomenon of that kind, is the contrast between the rigidity, the apparent lifelessness of the mountain, and this glorious manifestation of movement and life, the warm stream coming out of the mountain's side. Yet a moment's reflection will tell the traveler that the stern rigidity, the unmoving massiveness of the mountain is the direct physical cause of that entrancing spectacle of life. Through its lofty rigidity the mountain gathers the waters inside itself, and sends them out a very marvel of movement, light and life.

The height and unchangeable finality of our Christology are the total if remote cause of all the higher life in Christ that is to be found in souls. But the rigidity is merely apparent. There are in the doctrines of the Incarnation many aspects that proclaim the fundamental fact that God in becoming man meant it to be a transformation of man, soul and body.

We all believe in a general and vague way that God became man for the sake of man, for man's spiritual profit. But very few amongst us grasp the deeper truth, that the Incarnation is in itself, in its innermost nature, the highest possible uplifting of human nature, of mankind in general, at least potentially.

We then may consider the Incarnation in a twofold light. God becomes man, we say, for the sake of man. This may be something of the following kind. The God-Man, possessing infinitude of personal dignity, worth, and power, does something for the human race that uplifts and saves the race. His mission on earth is essentially to do that great thing to accomplish that great act, in the way, and under the circumstances, He knows best. It would be essentially a transient act, an act that might be dated and described by the historian as the act of man's redemption. We are orthodox Christians the moment we believe that God made man redeemed mankind by an act of His that took place here on earth.

But there is a second aspect to this most divine truth, a higher and more comprehensive aspect, which includes that first point of view, and which goes a good deal beyond. The redemption, says the man who is wise in the mystery of Christ, is more than a transient act on the part of the Son of God made man. The whole of the Son of God Incarnate is redemption, is the uplifting of the human nature.

The various phases and acts of Christ's career here on earth have but one object, to consummate Christ's fitness to be the redemption, to be mankind's uplifting.

> Of him (God) are you in Christ Jesus, who of God is made unto us wisdom, and justice, and sanctification, and redemption (1 Cor 1:30).

This deeper understanding of the mystery of Christ lays great stress on what the Son of God is, both in the divine and in the human element of Himself. The acts and facts of His life here on earth are infinitely precious to such people, be- cause they reveal the permanent character of the Son of God. It might even be said that they are precious, because they are known to have shaped permanently Christ's human character.

We have the Epistle to the Hebrews as an authority that Christ's human character received a lasting imprint from His earthly experiences:

> Whereas indeed he was the Son of God, he learned obedience by the things which he suffered. And being consummated, he became, to all that obey him, the cause of eternal salvation (Heb 5:8-9).

I might describe the two views as the verb view the substantive view. The first is the verb view of Christ's role; the second is the substantive view of it. One says, Christ *gives* life; the other says, Christ *is* life.

The two views, as already remarked, do not exclude each other, but they complete each other. It is, of course, a much greater thing to be life substantively, than merely to cause life, and when I say here that Christ is life substantively, I mean necessarily this, that He is the life of man substantively, not only life in Himself.

No one questions the expression that the Son of God is life in Himself. But what is so consoling is the ever recurring phraseology of the Scriptures, that the Son of God not only produces life in man, but is the life of man.

I select for the moment this one attribute of life for the sake of simplicity in my argumentation. Any other of Christ's roles and attributes might be instanced with the same degree of appropriateness.

The circumstance that the New Testament so constantly states Christ's relation to man in terms of substantives can never receive enough attention. Were such phraseology used even once it ought to rouse keenest interest in us. But it is not once, but hundreds of times that the inspired writers express themselves in such fashion when speaking of the share of man in the mystery of the Incarnation.

No one can fail to see the immense spiritual significance of such a turn of mind and speech in the sacred writers. Although the former, the Christian less educated, says a true thing when he professes his faith that Christ did redeem him, the latter speaks a much wiser and much more correct language when he says, Christ is my redemption.

For the first, redemption is a result, most gracious indeed, but it is something that came out of Christ; for the other, redemption is something inside Christ. He, too, feels redeemed, but his feelings are of a much higher nature, of a much diviner fiber.

And it is evident that the Incarnation becomes a much more glorious thing if the God Incarnate, instead of merely redeeming, is redemption itself. For once granted that God became man, that there is infinitude of power and sanctity in the God-Man, the work of redemption is no new marvel; it might be said to be child's play for the divine giant. But to be redemption, intrinsically, through His human nature, as well as through the divine element in Himself, is indeed a scope worthy of the One "Who was predestinated the Son of God in power according to the Spirit of sanctification" (ROM 1:4).

To do the great work for one who is Omnipotence is no new mystery. To be Himself life, light, food, happiness eternal, is a development of the initial mystery of the Hypostatic Union absolutely worthy of it.

The Son of God calls Himself the Resurrection and the Life, the Way, the Truth, the Light, the Beginning and the End. He is everything that renders man happy and holy, substantially and substantively.

It is the only mode of being man's Savior that really worthy of the Hypostatic Union, that the Incarnate God should be Salvation itself.

The aim and goal of the whole drama of the Incarnation, from the conception through the Holy Ghost in the Virgin's womb to the glories of the risen Jesus on the Easter morning is this, that the Man-God, Christ

Jesus, Son of God and Son of Mary, true God and true man, should be, both through His human as well as through His divine element, man's eternal life, and all the parts of that divine drama, with such a wonderful *dramatis persona* (person of the drama) in the center of it, are indispensable to that crowning achievement, that He, the Jesus of Nazareth, is man's life substantively, and not only life-giver to man.

To be life-giver needed no life-drama, such as the Gospel: it only needed God's innate and eternal omnipotence. But to be life to man necessitated a Christ, Who is the Son of God born of a Virgin, Who suffered under Pontius Pilate, Who died, was buried and rose again from the dead.

The Incarnation of Christian theology is indeed the personal union of Divinity with humanity. But let us always bear in mind that Incarnation, or Hypostatic Union, is still a general mystery, a mystery that could take place under other forms.

Thus any of the three Divine Persons could become incarnate. The personal union could have an Angel for its object, or any other human being, or even many other beings at the same time, either human or angelic.

In fact, no man knows under how many different conditions Hypostatic Union could take place. Thus Hypostatic Union need not at all include "the form of a slave," the abasement of the Christian Gospels. Hypostatic Union could be all a mystery of glory and happiness. But the Hypostatic Union that is the ground work of Christian spirituality is a Hypostatic Union of a well defined mode, deeply characterized and modified through its special purposes.

Through it the Son of God, the second Person of the Trinity, becomes man, assuming one individual human nature into the partnership of the Divine Personality with the specific purpose of becoming the higher life of that fallen man whose fall culminates in death.

To study the doctrines of the Incarnation without taking into account that very deep characterization is to miss the whole point. It would be like introducing some great personage into a dramatic play, without giving him a role or a character.

That God should become man is the first marvel; that God made man should be man's life, is the other marvel, as great as the first, in the sense in which a man's character is as great a thing as man's being.

III

The Role of Christ's Humanity

Before proceeding with the description of the Christian mind, I think it worth the reader's while to be given an opportunity of understanding more clearly the role of Christ's humanity, in being to man life, and resurrection, and all other things substantively.

It is the human nature, the human element in the Word Incarnate that gives to the Hypostatic Union its proper character, its traditional and wonderful individuality.

To explain all things that make up the riches of our redemption in Christ merely through the infinitude of the divine element in Jesus is a great practical error in the psychology of the Incarnation; Christ's humanity is as indispensable a part for His role as the Life of the world as is His divinity.

It is therefore of the utmost practical importance for the Christian Mind to have such views of the role of our Lord's humanity as to make that most sweet humanity the delight and the deepest object of our mental contemplation, so as to enable us to grasp at one glance the composite perfection of our new life in God, it being an indissoluble and inseparable blending of the Divine and the human.

A not uncommon phrase used with regard to Incarnation is this: Christ's humanity is said to have been totally absorbed by the Divinity in Him. What pious people mean generally when using such expression is that Christ's human nature has been brought so completely into line with the Divinity, has been made so absolutely subject to it, and has been sanctified by it so entirely, that it could never be to man an obstacle, when man wants to go directly to God through Christ. According to this view the Godhead in our Lord is so predominant, that practically His humanity is nowhere, and when you are in presence of the Lord, you are in presence of Divinity, pure and simple, for the practice of Christian contemplation.

This view considers Christ's humanity as being in a state of divine passiveness. It is a way of looking at our Lord frequently found in the beginnings of spiritual life, when the mind is for the first time overpowered by the thought of the all-sufficiency of God.

Such beginners, of course, hold more or less theoretically the Christian doctrine that all life and all grace and all redemption come through Christ's humanity as through a divinely appointed medium-ship: they know it to be the great element of mediation, though such knowledge does not render the humanity a living part of their thinking minds.

It is really a mental awkwardness in the beginner, an awkwardness resembling in some way the difficulties the Protestant mind has to find joy and rest in the thought that the Saints intercede for us with God. The Protestant mind sees in the Catholic position of the Saints in Heaven an obstacle between man's soul and God.

Now mature Christian sanctity suffers from no awkwardness of that kind. On the contrary, it exults in all things that come from God, and it never feels itself nearer to the fountainhead of all goodness than when it contemplates some wonderful created manifestation of God's creative love, and for mature sanctity God is at His best when He creates some wonderful being, giving it existence outside Himself.

And such is also the behavior of ripe wisdom in the mystery of Christ with regard to the humanity in the Incarnation. Far from considering Christ's humanity as having been absorbed by the Divinity, it rejoices at the thought that the humanity in Jesus is the highest and most potent expression of the Divinity. The Godhead, instead of absorbing it, brings it out, so to speak, with infinite effect.

Divinity communicates to humanity such potentialities, such vitalities, that no distinction need be made by our mind, as to what is the share of the one or the other in our redemption. It is an undivided result, and an undivided life, the divinized humanity, and the humanized Divinity, being the great life.

The Incarnation is adequately appreciated by those only to whom Christ's humanity is the marvel of marvels, a marvel in which they have their being, in which they live, work, die, and in which they hope to rise again from the dead, in which they find the fulness of the Godhead, as Moses found the fire in the bush.

The astonishing frailty of the human nature being made to flame forth the glory of eternal Godhead, and yet remaining unconsumed, and keeping its native greenness, is the ever refreshing anomaly of Christ's humanity.

> And the Lord appeared to him (Moses) in a flame of fire out of the midst of a bush: and he saw that the bush was on fire, and was not burnt. And Moses said, I will go and see this great sight why the bush is not burnt (Exod 3:2-3).

Far from considering Christ's humanity as having been absorbed by the divine element, the saint rejoices at the great discovery he is sooner or later privileged to make, that the ever blessed humanity is the highest, and the most active, and the most insistent expression of the Divinity; Hypostatic Union enhances its native realities in an infinite degree.

It is God's most astonishing production, it is the effect of what I may call super-creation, of an incomprehensibly high scale of perfection, a creation through which Divine personality is given to an individual nature, instead of an ordinary finite mode of existence. And although the saint knows that Christ's human nature is something that is inferior to the Divine nature in Him, he knows that this inferiority has been practically bridged over in the Hypostatic Union, that there are in that mystery such resources of life and power, that at no point are we in contact with anything, in our Lord, that does not bear the stamp of some infinitude, and there are no banks to that stream of life, which is Christ Jesus.

In sacred theology are contained the metaphysical principles that explain how, with the relative superiority of the divine element in our Lord over His humanity, this same humanity is yet a full and total cause of our higher life with God.

In our practical thinking we need not make any such distinction, just as we do not distinguish between a man's soul and a man's body when we think of some amiable person. We walk up bravely to that Person, Jesus, such as He stands before us, and we find Him to be infinite truth and infinite grace.

In all His manifestations, in the phases of His career, He is the one great wonder of heaven and earth, and our mind rejoices in Him exceedingly and endlessly.

> And evidently great is the mystery of godliness, which was manifested in the flesh, was justified in the spirit, appeared unto Angels, hath been preached unto the gentiles, is believed in the world, is taken up in glory (1 Tim 3:16).

IV

THE NECESSITY OF POSSESSING THE CHRISTIAN MIND

It was to be expected that a great philosophy of life would be built up on the fundamental facts of the Incarnation.

I do not pretend here that there actually exists in the history of Christian literature a complete and organic essay of that kind, undertaken specially with a view of evolving all the practical conclusions directly derived from the central fact of the Incarnation. To my knowledge there is no such book. But the life-philosophy of the Incarnation is none the less clear, none the less complete. It was apprehended intuitively by the Christian intellect, it was taken for granted at once, and it is stated by the Christian writers more as an obvious truth than as a theory of life.

St. Paul especially takes it all for granted, and because he takes it for granted he is our best authority on the subject. He sees at a glance how a practical question of life finds its solution in this main fact, that Christ, the Son of God, lived, died, and rose again from the dead.

According to St. Paul, the work of building up practically Christian life on the great foundation of the Incarnation is a work to be done by every Christian teacher, and a work in which one man is more successful than another.

According to the grace of God, that is given to me, as a wise architect, I have laid the foundation: and another buildeth thereon. But let every man take heed how he buildeth thereupon. For other foundation no man can lay, but that which is laid; which is Christ Jesus. Now if any man build upon this foundation, gold, silver, precious stones, wood, hay, stubble: every man's work shall be manifest: for the day of the Lord shall declare it, because it shall be revealed in fire (1 Cor 3:10-14).

But although the elements of the Christian mind are thus scattered through all the pages of Christian literature, practicality having been invariably responsible for the utterance of the writers, nevertheless it might not be outside the power of man to construct it all into one homogeneous whole.

In fact, if anything can be expected of the belief in the Incarnation, it is a philosophy of life, an attitude of the mind entirely and exclusively based on it. Both from its intrinsic principles, and from the utterances of those that have best experienced the powerful vitalities of the Incarnation, we ought to be able to construct a rule of life and thought so high, so comprehensive, and at the same time so workable, as to throw into the background all other human philosophies.

God was made man for the sake of man: such are our wonderful premises. "And I live, now not I: but Christ liveth in me" (Gal 2:20), is one of the many *a posteriori* axioms of the same verity. Who does not see at a glance what a magnificent theory of life could be built on such principles?

Say there were a man of great intellectual acumen, holding such truths only provisionally, what capital he could make out of them for a treatise on life! How much more we, to whom such phrases are the very truth of the eternal God!

In our own days thinking men have soared high in their efforts to put great distances between themselves and the soul killing miasmas of modern materialism. They have elaborated all kinds of etherial philosophies. There are the philosophies of the Mind, the philosophies of the Infinite, the philosophies of the Divine in man, the philosophies of the Absolute and so on.

They are pathetic efforts indeed, and a very good sign of the times in which we live; but one of their most interesting features is this, that many of them are ready to receive Christ, are houses that seem built just for such a guest as the Incarnate Son of God. What they call Mind, Infinite, Divine in man, Absolute, is an empty thing by itself, a house without an inhabitant, without any life in it. They are mere expressions of unlimited, undefined and indefinable longings.

But let Jesus of Nazareth be called Mind, as He is the Word of God; let Him be called Infinite, as in Him all fullness dwells; let Him be the Divine in man, being the Word made flesh; let Him be the Absolute, as He is the Alpha and the Omega; and you have a most perfect, a most heavenly philosophy, besides having a philosophy that is as true, as practical, as real, as a living person can be.

It would be a bad day, indeed, for Christianity, if, besides its divine *depositum* (deposit) of dogmas, it could not create in man a mental attitude, if it were barren of all philosophy, if it were not such as to enable the mind of man to read life, and the world, and the world's history in the light of the Incarnation, if the Christian doctrines had to be deposited as precious things in the very top story of the human mind, as ancient family heirlooms, whilst all the life, all the activity, all the practicality of the more active sections of our mental being were under the influence of systems of thought not begotten of the Incarnation.

Such a state of mind is a most dangerous limitation of the Kingdom of Christ. Christianity without a Christ philosophy of life, with the Son of God relegated to the upper chamber, while intellectual feasts and doings are going on below, is clearly a perilous state of tepidity for the baptized.

A Christian mind that could not move with the greatest ease "in Christ," finding Him a world of infinite interests and boundless perspectives, is indeed in a sorry plight. Whatever may be such a mind's reverence for the God Incarnate, it never knows exactly where to place Him, and what to make of Him, in the world-scheme.

It might well be objected that a living and practical philosophy of the Incarnation, as here postulated, could hardly be the achievement of the mind, even of a sincere Christian, without a special illumination, without a kind of personal revelation, which it is the lot of very few to possess. All our mind could possibly aspire to, it might be said, is a reverent acceptance of the mystery of the Incarnation, bowing before it, blindfolded and obedient. Is it not presumption to hope that one could train one's mind to think in terms of the Incarnation?

My answer is, that the acquisition of so glorious a mental attitude is a comparatively easy thing, and that it is an achievement possible with the ordinary graces given by God to His faithful.

There is first of all the Christian Mind *au fait* (by the way), in St. Paul, who is known and read in all the churches. To conform our minds to his, is not so much a process of mental deduction, as a direct influence, a direct contact of mind upon mind, as when we receive the warm effulgence of a great fire. It is not a reasoning, but a living participation of our minds in St. Paul's mind.

No doubt, in the case of St. Paul the mental illumination was entirely the gift of the Holy Ghost directly. But like all other productions of grace and genius once they are put forth, it becomes the natural dwelling place of all men's minds. Who could write a Shakespearean tragedy? Yet how many millions of minds have to be trained to think the thoughts and to assimilate the language of the great poet!

I do not admit that it is outside our range of progress to acquire the mental attitude here described, by an unceasing exercise of the mind and a constant contemplation of the principles of the Incarnation. Granted our faith in the Incarnation, and granted our knowledge of the more obvious axioms of theology, why should it be beyond us to think habitually in terms of the Incarnation?

God's grace is as ready to help our thinking, as it is prompt to support our acting. And if it ought to be every Christian's effort to do all things in Christ, why should we be debarred from thinking all our thoughts in Christ? Surely so great a phenomenon as the Incarnation is meant to modify deeply all human thinking under every possible aspect.

Christ is the Logos, the Word of God, the Wisdom of God. Through His very nature, He is meant to be the source of a mentality that is all His own.

V

SPECIAL CHRISTIAN MIND VERSUS GENERAL CHRISTIAN MIND

We may now consider more fully what is really meant by the Christian Mind.

As I have already observed, it is regrettable that we have no word in our language to enable us to speak of Christ in an adjective mode. The term Christian, both as a substantive and an adjective, refers not so much to Christ Himself, as to the believers in Christ, and things appertaining to them.

We ought to have a word which would make it possible for us to class under one adjective all things that are Christ's. The habit of calling things that are our Lord's very own "Christ things" has prevailed, the name itself having become an adjective. The title "Christ Mind" would be more descriptive of the purposes of this essay than its present superscription, "Christian Mind". But once more I give expression to the wish that there were an adjective term in our language to stand between the substantive name Christ, and the very comprehensive expression Christian.

There are only two complete mental systems in the history of human thought diametrically opposed and exhaustive of their subject. On the one hand we have Christian thought, and on the other we have monistic thought. All the other systems find their place within those two universal forms, as incomplete things are over-shadowed by those which are complete.

Monism has been worked out to its uttermost logical conclusions by those fearsome creatures, the German antichristian philosophers and professors of our days. Monism, as its name implies, makes it its fundamental principle that there is no distinction between Creator and creature. The world with all its phenomena is the evolution of one force. Even then, when Christian conclusions and monistic conclusions seem to coincide, the similarity is merely apparent.

Monism is radically and hopelessly the opposite of Christian thought. Christianism starts with the assumption of the real distinction between God and the world, between the Creator and creature, and the relations between the two, the Infinite Maker and the finite creature, come in everywhere in Christian thought. This is why Christian philosophy may be also called dualism, in direct opposition to monism, as it is an upholding of the distinction between the Creator and the created.

St. Thomas Aquinas may be considered as the most comprehensive exponent of the Christian dualism, though, of course, dualism is much less the work of a few well-known thinkers, than is monism. Dualism is really the common inheritance of mankind. Monism is a freak of darkness.

This philosophical digression will be helpful in our effort to define the scope of the Christian mind in the more restricted sense of this book.

In a very true sense, every sort of thinking that is not monism is Christian thinking, however it may be overlaid by error and confusion. The heathen who worships false gods is at bottom following out the principle of duality. He is certainly nearer to the kingdom of truth than the German monist.

On the other hand, Christian thought, Christian mind, in its general aspect, is every truth that is based ultimately on dualism; and antichristian thought, antichristian mind, is everything that rests on monism.

Christian mind, as the philosophical opposite of monism, is exceedingly vast and comprehensive. It implies certain views on religion, on politics, on economics, on science, on sociology, on eugenics, etc. Such views are simply called Christian, because they imply that the laws of the world, spiritual, moral, social, natural, are the property, so to speak, of an infinitely wise Creator, Who is not only the world's origin, but also the world's last court of appeal.

In this very general sense Christian thought differs in no wise from Jewish thought. Monism is its only real enemy. But the specific Christian Mind of which we are treating here may be said to be the opposite of Jewish thought in its post-messianic phase, for the Jew, whilst worshiping God, and whilst having the zeal of God, refuses to surrender his mind and his will to the higher manifestations of God found in the Incarnation.

With all his faith in God, he suffers from a lamentable ignorance of God, because he fails to understand the infinitely sweet mystery of God's love in the Incarnation:

> Jesus answered: If I glorify myself, my glory is nothing. It is my Father that glorifieth me, of whom you say that he is your God. And you have not known him: but I know him (JOHN 8:54).

Christian Mind, in our restricted sense, is not so much a specific view of the world and its laws, as of God and His free favors. It presupposes all the general Christian thinking, but rises infinitely higher. The general Christian law of morality is the groundwork from which it soars. Christian Mind, therefore, may be best defined as the attitude of man's mind caused directly and totally by the Incarnation.

It is to the general Christian view of things, to dualism, what Paul the Apostle is to Saul the Pharisee. Saul the Pharisee saw the world in God. Paul the Apostle sees both God and the world in Christ Jesus. It is an immense uplifting of the mind, so great an uplifting indeed that to many it seems an entire upheaval, and it is dreaded and hated as an upheaval.

It is one of the characteristics of the Christian Mind to be so totally misunderstood by the Ordinary religious mind of the orthodox believers in

God and His works, as to make the extermination of it an apparent service rendered unto God.

> They will put you out of the synagogues: yea, the hour cometh, that, whosoever killeth you, will think that he doth a service to God (JOHN 16:2).

The question will be asked here how then the general Christian mind ranges itself under the special Christian Mind, the outcome of the Incarnation. For it is unthinkable that our mental perspective should be subdivided into regions. We must see all things as lying within one plane, bounded by one horizon. Our plane is Christ, the horizon is Christ's human nature.

All things that are must be visible in Christ, for the Christian Mind. The great doctrine of the Word gives us the key.

> All things were made by him: and without him was made nothing that was made (JOHN 1:3).

The Word made flesh is universal power, universal harmony, universal wisdom made flesh. We cannot dissociate Christ from the things of nature that are true and beautiful. Christ is truly the "heir of the world" (ROM 4:13).

There is no greater privilege for the Christian Mind than to view all things in the sweet glow of the God Incarnate, besides having the blessed vision of the Hypostatic Union itself.

This containment of all things in the God made man will be more fully developed as the book goes on. But I thought it wise to say a word here as to the relative position of what I call here the general Christian mind, and the noble thing that will now claim all our attention, the Christian Mind.

VI

A Short Criticism of the Mental Attitude of Christians

*A*s Christianity implies everything that is good and true, a man may be a sincere professor of the Christian faith without actually exhibiting in his life that special mental attitude, the Christian Mind, which is the object of this book.

It is, of course, obvious that no one has a right to call himself a Christian unless he believes sincerely that all his spiritual hopes are based on the Incarnation. But it is quite possible for any of us to hold such a faith, to lead good and godly lives, and yet to remain mentally outside the mystery of the living Christ, to go through life without ever having experienced the truth of maxims like the following:

For to me, to live is Christ: and to die is gain (Phil 1:21).

It is so very easy even for the faithful Christian to order his life merely according to the rules of that general Christian mentality which is the opposition of materialism and infidelity, including always at least a theoretical acceptance of the Redemption in Christ.

It is perhaps more difficult for the Catholic not to enter at least a few steps into the mystery of the Son of God, as the Catholic is bound to make use of the Sacraments, which are the most palpable way of being in touch with the Risen Son of God. It might seem difficult that a man who receives with faith and devoutness the Bread of Life, should not go beyond a merely theoretical acceptance of the life in Christ, for spiritual purposes. Yet it must be confessed that even for a Catholic, with the habitual use of the Sacraments, the Christian Mind is many times conspicuous by its absence. For him the Sacraments are essentially helps towards moral goodness; and so they are, though they are something vastly greater. By far the greatest quantity of Christian literature is based not on the specific, but on the general Christian mind. If we are within reach of a library in which "spiritual books" abound we can easily verify this assertion.

Let us take for instance the virtue of temperance, in its classical meaning of purity of life. From Tertullian, through Cassian, through St. Thomas Aquinas and Rodriguez, down to Father Maturin in our own days, the virtue is described in terms mostly philosophical, terms which any man who is not a Nietzschan must accept. Now and then Christ's example is pressed into service. But the exhortations to temperance are such that no sensible pagan can jeer at them. Every possible philosophic system with any claim to intellectual respectability is ransacked and quoted in support of the virtue. It is indeed a most complete economy in *nova et vetera* (new and old things).

Against this very general view of the virtue or temperance we have St. Paul's own experience and statement of it.

> Let us walk honestly as in the day: not in rioting and drunkenness, not in chambering and impurities, not in contention and envy. But put ye on the Lord Jesus Christ, and make not provision for the flesh on its concupiscences (ROM 13:13-14).

The Christian temperance in opposition to pagan profligacy is made clear to us in one magnificent phrase: "Put ye on the Lord Jesus Christ."

Far be it from me to say that the Fathers and preachers of all times ignored such a view of Christian temperance, or that they never made allusion to it. The preacher and the writer through the very nature of their profession go after diffusion of thought. But the prophet who speaks God's own words discards diffusion, and utters truth in its highest and most concentrated form.

Virtue is rendered amiable to us from a thousand different points of view, in the written and spoken word of all centuries. But when everything has been said, when every facet of man's mind has been irradiated by the beauty of temperance, there is still a higher concept, a milder light, a statement of the truth that makes all other statements appear as mere childish prattle: "Put ye on the Lord Jesus Christ."

Every other point of Christian life could be made the object of similar study.

The whole of Catholic morality has been cast into the mould of Aristotelian philosophy by the great monk and thinker St. Thomas Aquinas. The Greek genius and the medieval friar meet and make friends. And it is only men who have never taken the trouble of studying the great *Summa*, in the *Prima Secundae* and *Secunda Secundae*, who could dare to accuse St. Thomas of having fettered the principles of Christian ethics, of having curtailed the liberties of the children of God.

The ethics of St. Thomas are the most liberal, the most generous, the most practical ethics in the world. Yet in all their beauty and generosity, they are no more than an adumbration of the heavenly born ethics of the Incarnation, thus described by St. Paul in his own person:

> According to the justice that is in the Law, (I was) conversing without blame. But the things that were gain to me, the same I have counted loss for Christ. Furthermore I count all things to be but loss, for the excellent knowledge of Jesus Christ my Lord: for whom I have suffered the loss of all things, and count them but as dung, that I may gain Christ: And may be found in him not having my justice, which is of the Law, but that which is of the faith of Christ Jesus, which is of God, justice in faith. That I may know him, and the power of his resurrection, and the fellowship of his sufferings,

being made conformable to his death. If by any means I may attain to the resurrection which is from the dead (Phil 3:6-16).

The services of the general Christian mind are incalculable. They give satisfaction to man's reasoning powers. They produce a kind of mental well-being that comes from the fullness of truth. To neglect the general Christian mind would be the greatest error: it would imply a kind of contempt of one of the laws of spiritual life, the law of the liberty of the children of God. At the same time there could be no greater danger for the Christian cause than an attempt to express Christian life only in philosophical, legal, or even canonical terms, and to consider such expressions as exhaustive of the subject.

The fellowship of Christ's passion and resurrection will always defy definition. It is something higher than thought and law.

The general Christian mind and the special Christian Mind are not two opposites; on the contrary they complete each other:

Do not think that I come to destroy the law, or the prophets. I am not come to destroy, but to fulfill (Matt 5:17).

No man ever saw the things of Christ more clearly since the days of St. Paul than did St. Francis of Assisi. In the possession of the Son of God all other things of mind were as nothing to him. In that great love of the Son of God he gathered together his disciples. But even Francis very soon learned that he could not dispense with the less living elements of canon law and ecclesiastical authority. The stern Roman canonists did him great service in protecting the fervor which he had brought into the world from becoming unruly.

At a later period St. Teresa of Avila, whose mind was full of the Son of God, if ever human mind was, professed her indebtedness and her admiration for the unemotional scholastic theologians who gave her the assurance that her intuitions of divine things were in perfect conformity with the reasoned theories of Catholic philosophy and theology.

On the other hand, to live merely by reasoned systems of spirituality, however perfect, would be the greatest disaster to the Church. It would mean law without love, power without meekness, authority without the softening influence of paternity, intellectual keenness without humility, zeal for God without knowledge of God's true character.

A spiritual life that is not a reproduction of the life of Christ will sooner or later become a dangerous mistake, all the more dangerous as it is so brilliant. Happy are we, if we live at a period of Christian history when the mystical knowledge and love of the Son of God go hand in hand with sound thinking and wise government.

VII

St. Paul's Mind

The specific Christian Mind is essentially mystical, in the modern sense of the word: that is to say, it is the possession and intuition of a great spiritual fact, whose reality is greater than anything the mind can acquire by its own reasoning powers. It is a reality that is overwhelmingly present; it transcends classifications and definitions, though containing them implicitly.

St. Paul is the greatest mystic of all times, because he apprehended Christ's personality so mightily, and read all things in Him so clearly and directly. All the minor realities of human life are to him law. But when there comes the newly found reality of life, Christ, law disappears, Christ alone remains, and all life, big and small, he reads now in terms of Christ.

Before expounding the more positive elements of the Christian Mind, I intend stating its more critical aspect by following St. Paul in his wonderful analysis of the respective values of the law and the living Christ.

We are all familiar with the well-worn antithesis that opposes the old law to the new law. We hear it constantly said that the old law was a state of servitude, whilst the new law is a state of superabundant grace. The antithesis is a true rendering of spiritual facts, and above all, it has the consecration of Ecclesiastical usage. But I doubt whether St. Paul would have liked it as a theological phrase. Certainly it does not come from him.

It is against St. Paul's genius to think of the new era that came with Christ as a law, however pure and lofty, and nowhere do we find him stating this opposition between the old law and the new law. For him the law is simply abrogated, it is dead, as dead as the dead Christ on the cross, with this difference however, that the dead Christ rose again, whilst the law is not meant to rise. It is dead and buried and condemned, forever.

The new state of things is not a law, not a system, it is the living God Himself, it is the risen Christ. The antithesis of St. Paul is not between the old law and the new law, but between law and grace, between law and Christ:

> You are not under the law, but under grace (ROM 6:14).

> You also are become dead to the law by the body of Christ: that you may belong to another, who is risen again from the dead (ROM 7:4).

It is true that once or twice the Apostle uses the term law in connection with the new dispensation:

> The law of the spirit-of-life, in Christ Jesus, hath delivered me from the law of sin and death (ROM 8:2).

> Bear ye one another's burdens: and so you shall fulfill the law of Christ (GAL 6:2).

In both these instances the term law has an almost ironical meaning, as it denotes things that are essentially not matters for a law. So it may be asserted safely that the common antithesis be- tween the old law and the new law is by no means a Pauline idea, as for him the Incarnation and its grace could never be encompassed within legal concepts, even of the loftiest order.

Christ the Son of the living God stands before Paul as the essence of Christian sanctity. The concept of Christ Himself being all law and all religion, may be rightly called St. Paul's central spiritual fact. In order to establish it firmly, the Apostle wrote more on this subject than on any other. He lays a regular siege to the Jewish as well as to the heathen mind that he may convince it of the all-important truth that the Son of God, made man, and crucified for man, has become man's spiritual life.

The Epistle to the Romans, the one to the Galatians, large sections of the Epistles to the Corinthians, the Colossians, and the Philippians, would be incomprehensible if we did not read them in the light of that great Pauline idea, that Christ Himself is spiritual life.

Before proceeding, let me put more clearly the practical distinction embodied in St. Paul's' view of Christ's role in man's higher life. One might consider spiritual life as a thing perfect in itself, for whose realization and attainment every sort of supernatural help is given us, the greatest help being the Incarnation, and all that it involves. Or one might, on the other hand, consider the Incarnate God as possessing all finality, and spiritual life being a road to Him, He Himself, in His own Person, being the goal.

The first view makes of spiritual life the end and of the Incarnation a means towards that end. The second view, on the contrary, makes the Incarnation, or the Incarnate God, the aim, and spiritual life, or the practice of all justice, the means towards finding Him. It is evident that the two views differ profoundly, and must in practice affect deeply the soul's movements.

St. Paul will not rest content until he has destroyed in our minds the last vestige that gives any finality to anything, however holy, outside Christ. St. Paul has the unsparing anger of the man with generous disposition, who has had his soul cramped for a long time by a spiritual system of inferior merit, that had been given to him as the highest perfection, and whose defects he had cherished in his former enthusiasm as much as its good points.

He has found out his mistake: he sees now how crushed he had been, and there are no bounds to his indignation. The inferior system that had made his soul an unconscious slave, was the law, the old law of Moses. It had kept him and his people from Christ. His denunciations of that law now are as strong as they are varied in character.

His mind finds endless stratagems to break down that intellectual wall which kept men from immediate and personal contact with the Son of the living God, and a short description of the main line of attack on that pernicious practical error will be, I trust, as useful to the reader as it is interesting.

The objection might be made, at this stage, that St. Paul's rancors and indignations were directed indeed against the law of Moses, with its material burdens, and that we are not justified in reading into his utterances that higher and much more subtle distinction between Christ's Person and general spiritual life, a distinction described a moment ago. But let me give at once the assurance that this higher substitution of the living Son of God for a system of spirituality is contained in St. Paul's main idea.

The law of Moses represented to the mind of St. Paul the whole system of justice' and spirituality known to man up to the glorious advent of Life itself.

VIII

St. Paul's Argumentations

In order to arrive at that most consoling conclusion, that Christ is our higher life, St. Paul's mind travels over very picturesque and, one might almost say, over very wild ground.

Or, to be more accurate, to St. Paul the great truth had come like a flash of lightening: it transformed him into a being of light and joy, in the twinkling of an eye. It is the Jew and the Gentile, and more the Jew than the Gentile, he takes over the picturesque and rugged circuits of his theological argumentations, and he drops them, panting with effort, at Christ's feet and he tells them: "Here is the source for you of the living waters."

I think it worth the reader's while to go over St. Paul's strange and quaint reasonings, for I am afraid that many a student of the Scriptures has an unconscious prejudice against those very passages in St. Paul's writings; he thinks them too exclusively rabbinic in their concept and their drift. He might be tempted to consider them as having no longer any actuality, since the controversies which gave rise to them did not survive the first Christian ages.

No mistake could be more fatal. Those rugged efforts of St. Paul's intellect are the wild rock and the hard tree where we find the purest spiritual honey: I mean that sweetest of all truths, that Christ Himself is our Life.

I take the various arguments in the order in which they are found in the Epistles, beginning with the Epistle to the Romans. I shall not always quote the full text, but give the meaning of the passages as a free paraphrase.

The fourth chapter of the Epistle to the Romans takes us back to the heroic days of the Jewish nation, to the calm and simple days when God made a compact of friendship with Abraham. The great old patriarch was without a son. It was the one shadow in a life full of sunshine. Even when God came near to him in a vision, and spoke to him words of comfort, the humble patriarch turned round to the Lord and told Him fearlessly that without a son the kind words of the Lord were no full consolation:

> Now when these things were done, the word of the Lord came to Abram by vision, saying: Fear not, Abram, I am thy protector, and thy reward exceedingly great. And Abram said: Lord God, what wilt thou give me? I shall go without children: and the son of the steward of my house is this Damascus Eliezer. And Abram added: But to me thou hast not given seed: and lo my servant, born in my house, shall be my heir. And immediately the word of the Lord came to him, saying: He shall not be thy heir; but he that shall come out of thy bowels, him shalt thou have for thy heir. And he brought him forth abroad, and said to him: Look up to heaven and number the stars, if thou canst. And he said to him: So shall thy seed be. Abram believed God, and it was reputed to him for justice (GEN 15:1-6).

This glorious promise on the part of God, a promise that includes the future Messiah amongst the seed of Abraham, is a most gratuitous advance on the part of God. It came directly from the mouth of Jehovah as a token of personal friendship and unprovoked liberality. Abraham, on his side, rose to the height of those divine advances. He believed in the promise without a moment's hesitation.

"Against hope", says St. Paul,

> he believed in hope; that he might be made the father of many nations. ... And he was not weak in faith; neither did he consider his own body now dead, whereas he was almost an hundred years old, nor the dead womb of Sara. In the promise also of God he staggered not by distrust; but was strengthened in faith, giving glory to God: Most fully knowing that whatsoever he has promised, he is able also to perform. And therefore it was reputed to him unto justice (Rom 4:18-22).

Abraham's supreme spiritual merit lay in this most generous and most unquestioning reliance on God's friendship. This act of perfect trust in God made Abraham the just man par excellence. "It was reputed to him unto justice."

St. Paul keeps on reiterating the gratuitousness of Abraham's privilege. Abraham's spiritual elevation comes from his meeting God's loving advances so wholeheartedly. God, on the other hand, makes those advances freely, not as a reward of any special works on the part of the patriarch: above all, true and faithful observance of the law could not be credited with such recognition at God's hands.

The law of Moses did not exist yet, and circumcision itself, the primary article of the law, had not yet been imposed on Abraham. The whole of that manifestation of divine friendship is not only superior to the law, it took place long before the law was established:

> For not through the law was the promise to Abraham, or to his seed, that he should be heir of the world, but through the justice of faith (Rom 4:13).

Once more, God and Abraham meet directly, and their compact is as a compact between mutual friends.

But all this subtle analysis of Abraham's privilege is meant to lead to the following conclusion, which states the Christ spirituality in such uncompromising language:

> Now it is not written only for him, that it was reputed to him unto justice. But also for us, to whom it shall be reputed, if we believe in him, that raised up Jesus Christ, our Lord, from the dead. Who was delivered up for our sins, and rose again for our justification (ROM 4:23-26).

From the uncovenanted and unsystematized privileges and graces and virtues of Abraham, St. Paul leaps on to the still higher liberties of the Christian. Christ's resurrection, and our practical faith in that resurrection, bring us nearer to the living God, "who calleth those things that are not, as those that are" (ROM 4:17), than Abraham's unwavering trust in God's promise that a son would be granted to him, though "he was almost a hundred years old" (4:19).

It is the same spirit of the liberty of the children of God, and the risen Christ, more than Abraham's overjoyed fatherhood, that is the real sign of God's love for the elect. No law however perfect, no covenant however sacred, can come up in spiritual perfection to that most personal token of divine friendship, the risen Christ. It is the Christian's matchless advantage that life with the risen Christ sums up, or rather takes the place of, all God's covenants, just as with Abraham the honors of a glorious fatherhood represent all that the Lord God is to him.

The thought occurred very soon to St. Paul, as it must, of course, to every thinking man, that this absolute superiority to law, in virtue of Christ's personal friendship, enjoyed by the Christian, would lead to a kind of contempt of the law, and that the liberty of the Incarnation would be turned into a disregard of the ordinary moral precepts. In his effort to rebut the objection he plunges into a new consideration, which on the one hand saves him from a dangerous antinomianism, and which on the other hand is still a more brilliant exposition of his absorbing theme, the all-sufficiency of Christ, as a principle of sanctity.

I give it as the second argument, and instead of being borrowed from the Jewish history, it is taken from the beginnings of Christian life, baptism. The sixth chapter to the Romans opens with it:

> What shall we say then? shall we continue in sin that grace may abound? God forbid. For we, that are dead to sin, how shall we live any longer therein? Know ye not that all we, who are baptized in Christ Jesus, are baptized in his death? For we are buried together with him by baptism into death: that, as Christ is risen from the dead by the glory of the Father, so we also may walk in newness of life. For if we have been planted together in the likeness of his death, we shall be also in the likeness of his resurrection. Knowing this, that our old man is crucified with him, that the body of sin may be destroyed, to the end that we may serve sin no longer. For he that is dead is justified from sin. Now if we be dead with Christ, we believe that we shall live also together with Christ: Knowing that Christ, rising again from the dead, dieth no more, death shall no more have dominion over him. For in that he died to sin, he died once; but in that he liveth, he liveth unto God: So do you also reckon that you are dead to sin, but alive unto God in Christ Jesus our Lord. Let not sin therefore reign in your mortal body, so as to obey the lusts thereof. Neither yield ye your members as instruments of iniquity unto sin; but present yourselves to God as those that are alive from the dead, and your members as instruments of justice unto God (Rom 6:13).

I have transcribed the whole passage, as no paraphrase could do justice to such words.

Here, more than anywhere else, one cannot help feeling sad at the thought that our minds are so little in tune with that Infinite, which is Christ, that passages like the one just quoted have a very unfamiliar ring for our cold and critical intellects. We fail to perceive the superhuman logic of St. Paul's discourse. Being so badly instructed in the mystery of Christ, and in the mystery of baptismal regeneration, we are unable to make of such language our own rules of thinking and speaking. The death, then, of Christ, and baptism, are the same spiritual reality. Our own higher life, again, and Christ's resurrection, are the same spiritual realities.

The Christian detests sin, is dead to sin, not in virtue of a law that says: "Thou shalt not", but in virtue of his keen realization of Christ's death, Who died on the cross to destroy sin. Through the innermost fibers of his regenerated being the death of Christ makes him have a horror of sin.

Why does he want a law to forbid sin, when he sees that Christ died from the evil of man's sin? Such a sight, the sight of the crucified Son of God, is warning enough for the Christian: it is more than warning, it is a permanent state of conscience that makes sin appear in its full hideousness. And how does he ever want to go back to sin, when it is his very condition to walk with the risen Christ in newness of life?

It is possible, of course, for the Christian to commit grievous sin. But his whole spiritual being, built up on Christ's death and Christ's resurrection, simply cries out against that deed in a way that law never can do. His sin is against his own regenerated soul, much more than against a law. Far from opening the door to antinomianism, St. Paul's central doctrine kills sin, and gives birth to sanctity long before law speaks.

The death of Christ, and the resurrection of Christ are much more powerful guardians of purity than mere precepts. They are the temperament of the Christian soul, and are infinitely more sensitive than mere knowledge of duty.

> So do you also reckon that you are dead to sin, but alive unto God in Christ Jesus our Lord (ROM 6:11).

Could there be a better description of the Christ psychology, of the all-sufficiency of Christ, as the principle of spiritual life?

The general idea of the substitution of Christ for the system of law, and the more special idea that such a substitution is a quickening of the moral sense, far from its being an open door to antinomianism, are illustrated by one and the same example, at the beginning of the seventh chapter in 1 Corinthians. It is the third argument.

The law that governs matrimony, like all law, has dominion over man as long as he lives. Therefore, if the husband dies, the woman is free to be with another man: had she acted thus in the life-time of her husband, she would indeed have been an object of general reprobation.

Now Christ died: man is free from the law that yoked him down before that great event, the death of Christ. Man is free to be another's; he is no longer the law's. And whose is he now? Now he belongs to the risen Christ, in order "that we may bring forth fruit to God" (ROM 7:4).

For this liberty to go away from the law, to be with another, is not a forgetfulness of duty, it is not a barrenness in spirit, but it is fruitfulness in God Himself. It is the higher matrimony of the soul with God, and if it is a service, it is "in the newness of spirit, not in the oldness of the letter."

I now transcribe the whole text, ROM 7:1-7:

> Know you not, brethren (for I speak to them that know the law), that the law hath dominion over a man, as long as he liveth? For the woman that hath an husband, whilst her husband liveth is bound to the law. But if her husband be dead, she is loosed from the law of her husband. Therefore, whilst her husband liveth, she shall be called an adulteress, if she be with another man; but if her husband be dead, she is delivered from the law of her husband: so that she is not an adulteress, if she be with another man. Therefore, my brethren, you also are become dead to the law, by the body of Christ: that you may belong to another, who is risen again from the dead, that we may bring forth fruit to God. For when we were in the flesh, the passions of sin which were by the law, did work in our members to bring forth fruit unto death. But now we are loosed from the law of death, wherein we were detained: so that we should serve in the newness of spirit, not in the oldness of the letter.

The two main ideas come out very clearly from this apparently twisted, but very telling, simile. The soul leaves the law, now dead, and is wedded to the risen Christ, and the natural fruit or this happy and loving alliance is spiritual fecundity.

I must remind the reader that I do not profess to be writing a commentary on the Epistles of St. Paul, but am concerned with the study of his Christ psychology. Were I to write such a commentary, I would give very special attention to St. Paul's way of using metaphors and similes. The Apostle never uses a parable in the logical sequel, of a Gospel parable, for instance; for him, an example is not a thing of logic and sequel, but it is above all thing of mental contacts.

Between the great truth that overwhelms his mind, and a given example from history, or from law or from nature, he perceives points of contact, and his mind jumps from one point of contact to another irrespective of reasoned connections.

So in this instance. Death of the husband means liberty for the wife. Christ also is another man in His risen state from what He was in death. And those things which follow concerning the new fruitfulness in God, are so many sparks of light, scintillating forth from St. Paul's mind, as it works upon its simile of the wedding with the risen Christ, and as it sees new points of contact.

It would be quite futile to press St. Paul's comparison beyond what it really is, a brilliant assemblage of points of contact. No amount of subtlety could ever make of Christ's death the logical parallel of a husband's death, for the simple reason that the soul was not wedded to Christ before His death. But the great fact remains, that Christ's death has set man free from sin and servitude, even from spiritual servitude, and through the merit of that death we are entitled to the unspeakably high grace of the spiritual nuptials of the soul with the risen Christ, we are called to serve in the newness of spirit, not in the oldness of the letter.

The living spirit, as opposed to the dead letter, is one of St. Paul's ever recurring ideas, and the relation of this idea with what I might call Christ-

spirituality is obvious: Christ is the living spirit, everything else is a dead letter.

Paul has drunk so deep from the cup of Christ's love, that the wisest and the best thing, when not informed by Christ's presence, is dull and dead to him. In the second Epistle to the Corinthians we find him quite unexpectedly giving utterance to this obsessing thought, with reference to a matter that seemed hardly fit to furnish an occasion for so noble an utterance.

His enemies had been trying to undermine his position at Corinth; he appeals to their old affection and to his own well known affection for them. With contempt he spurns away the idea that he is trying to commend himself to their favor, after so many years of loyal love. He is not the man who is in need of an epistle of commendation to them, a letter of introduction!

The word "epistle of commendation," coming here as a natural development of his eager effort to show his real footing with the Corinthians, is an idea. too full of bright facets to be neglected. What need has he of a letter? Are not the Corinthians written large over the Apostle's heart, and are not they a letter which the whole Church can read? And more still, are not the Corinthians an epistle written by Christ Himself, ministered by Paul, who is Christ's amanuensis, a letter written not with ink, but with the spirit of the living God, not in tables of stone, but in fleshly tables of the heart?

And this close personal relation of Christ with the converts and of the converts with St. Paul, gives him, St. Paul, great confidence, as he knows himself to be a fit minister of the New Testament, not in the letter but in the spirit:

> Do we begin again to commend ourselves? Or do we need (as some do) epistles of commendation to you, or from you? You are our epistle, written in our hearts, which is known and read by all men: Being manifested, that you are the epistle of Christ, ministered by

us, and written not with ink, but with the Spirit of the living God: not in tables of stone, but in the fleshly tables of the heart. And such confidence we have, through Christ towards God. Not that we are sufficient to think anything of ourselves, as of ourselves: but our sufficiency is from God. Who also hath made us fit ministers of the new testament, not in the letter, but in the spirit. For the letter killeth, but the spirit quickeneth. Now if the ministration of death, engraven with letters upon stones, was glorious: so that the children of Israel could not steadfastly behold the face of Moses, for the glory of his countenance which is made void: How shall not the ministration of the Spirit be rather in glory (2 Cor 3:1-8)?

It would be impossible to find anywhere a more vivacious use of a metaphor, where there is such an absolute disregard of the logical parallelism combined with so complete an effect as to the final impression. We know, when we have read the passage, that St. Paul has once more spoken his great conviction, that Christ is the living spirit.

The underlying metaphorical idea is a letter of commendation, the metaphor reaches its climax when the writer makes the assertion that the Corinthians themselves are a letter written by Christ "in fleshly hearts" by the Spirit of the Living God. It would be difficult to express in a more telling way, that the psychology of the Christian is something quite unique, something that is very personal to Christ: "Being manifested, that you are the epistle of Christ." The regenerated soul bears Christ's private signature.

In his metaphor of the commendatory letter, St. Paul, quite unexpectedly again, introduces the allusion to the tables of stone on which the law had been written, in opposition to "the fleshly tables of the heart." He rises easily to the parallel of Moses, who carried the tables, and to the countenance of Moses, which was so shining in power that the children of Israel did not dare to look upon it.

This new thought, the glorious face of Moses that is veiled, is one more welcome illustration, by way of contraries, of the excellency of the Christian ministry (which ministry is merely another side of the Christian relations with Christ). It leads up to one of the most striking pronouncements even from St. Paul, on the immediateness of our relations with our Lord:

> Now the Lord is a Spirit, and where the Spirit of the Lord is, there is liberty. But we all beholding the glory of the Lord with open face, are transformed into the same image from glory to glory, as by the Spirit of the Lord (2 COR 3:17-18).

Frequently these beautiful words are quoted as being a description of the blessed vision of God in Heaven. Such interpretation can be read into them, by way of extension, but there is no doubt that the words refer to the process of spiritual identification between Christ and man, here on earth.

The whole context demands that we should apply the doctrine to our present life. It is in the present life we enjoy the privileges, the glories of that higher ministry, which has finality, in opposition to the Mosaic dispensation which is made void in Christ. As the minister of a God who speaks with us directly, the Apostle disdains to put a veil over his face in his daily intercourse with the faithful.

Let every Christian gaze constantly and boldly on the face of Christ.

Nothing stands between the Son of God and the soul, nothing can stand between, as "the Lord is a Spirit" who is not tied down to any circumstance of time and place, of laws and ceremonies:

> Now if the ministration of death, engraven with letters upon stones, was glorious: so that the children of Israel could not steadfastly behold the face of Moses, for the glory of his countenance, which is made void: How shall not the ministration of the Spirit be rather in glory? For if the ministration of condemnation be glory, much more the ministration of justice aboundeth in glory. For even that which was glorious in this part was not glorified, by reason of the glory that excelleth. For if that which is done away was glorious,

much more that which remaineth is in glory. Having therefore such hope, we use much confidence: And not as Moses put a veil upon his face that the children of Israel might not steadfastly look on the face of that which is made void. But their senses were made dull. For until this present day, the selfsame veil, in the reading of the old testament, remaineth not taken away (because in Christ it is made void). But even until this day when Moses is read, the veil is upon their heart. But when they shall be converted to the Lord, the veil shall be taken away. Now the Lord is a Spirit. And where the Spirit of the Lord is, there is liberty. But we all beholding the glory of the Lord with open face, are transformed into the same image from glory to glory, as by the Spirit of the Lord (2 Cor 3:7-15).

The Epistle to the Galatians, more than any other epistle, of set purpose, is the defense of the doctrine that "as many of you as have been baptized in Christ, have put on Christ" (Gal 3:27).

The Galatians, instructed and baptized by St. Paul, directly from Paganism, had lent their ear to false teachers, who made them believe that the law of Moses was indispensable to salvation. St. Paul rebukes their simplicity with the masterfulness of a loving and watchful father.

The whole epistle is about the law versus the living Christ: directly and primarily he means the law of Moses, but, as in many other places, he extends his doctrines, and he applies his argumentations to the moral law in general, and he contrasts it with the advantage of having one's higher hopes anchored in the living Christ.

The epistle contains some of St. Paul's most famous and most characteristic sayings, embodying his great spiritual experience of the all-sufficiency of Christ. It is there we come on his immortal profession of life in Christ:

> God forbid that I should glory, save in the cross of our Lord Jesus Christ; by whom the world is crucified to me, and I to the world (Gal 6:14).

But those glowing tributes to the all-sufficiency of Christ will be made object of a special study. At present I am concerned with the analysis of the arguments, mostly metaphorical, by means of which St. Paul drives home the great truth.

There are three distinct argumentations towards that object in this epistle.

First, the Apostle gives a new and abridged version of the great argument we have already seen in the Epistle to the Romans. It is all about the promise made to Abraham. The whole strength of the argumentation lies in the nature of a promise. It was not a bilateral compact, but an unilateral one, God alone making a promise.

Now a mediator is not of one; but God is one (Gal 3:20).

The law was a bilateral arrangement between God and man, and Moses had been the mediator between God and the people.

The covenant that came after (it was 431 years after) could not weaken that great promise. The law cannot give life, if it did the great promise of God concerning the seed, which is Christ, would have become superfluous.

"That the promise by faith of Jesus Christ might be given to them that believe" (Gal 3:22) is just the Christian's hope. He stands and falls with the reliability of that personal, unilateral act of God, a promise.

The Church in her liturgy makes of nearly the whole of this passage the Epistle of the Thirteenth Sunday after Pentecost. Reading it here will bring home familiar words, though we may have heard the epistle many times, sincerely wondering what place it occupied in our supernatural outfit:

> Brethren: To Abraham were the promises made and to his seed. He saith not, And to his seeds, as of many: but as of one, And to thy seed, which is Christ. Now this I say, that the testament which was confirmed by God, the law which was made after four hundred and thirty years, doth not disannul, to make the promise of no effect. For if the inheritance be of the law, it is no more of promise.

But God gave it to Abraham by promise. Why then was the law? It was set because of transgressions, until the seed should come, to whom he made the promise, being ordained by angels in the hand of a mediator. Now a mediator is not of one: but God is one. Was the law then against the promises of God? God forbid. For if there had been a law given which could give life, verily justice should have been by the law. But the scripture hath concluded all under sin, that the promise by the faith of Jesus Christ might be given to them that believe. But before the faith came, we were kept under the law shut up, unto that faith which was to be revealed (GAL 3:16-23).

The last sentence, containing the metaphor of children shut up under tutorship — for such is the meaning of the verse — gives rise in St. Paul's mind to a new and very beautiful simile, the simile of the pedagogue. The law is a mere pedagogue, our pedagogue in Christ: faith sets us free from the pedagogue's tutorship, and makes us children of God.

All men are equally privileged through baptism, they are all one in Christ Jesus. The spiritual condition of the Christian is absolutely superior to any other state of morality, and the soul of the Christian enjoys an endless measure of spiritual liberty.

The metaphor is worked out more consecutively than most other metaphors of St. Paul, and the climax of the reasoning is reached quite naturally, culminating as it does in the glorious and well known words:

And because you are sons, God hath sent the Spirit of His Son into your hearts, crying: Abba, Father (GAL 4:6).

Before quoting the full text, I should like to call the reader's attention to the third verse of the fourth chapter, where St. Paul speaks of the condition that preceded the Incarnation as follows:

So we also, when we were children, were in bondage under the elements of the world (GAL 4:3).

The Christian's liberation is indeed a deliverance from the elements of the world, as he is superior, through his faith, to the merely natural exigencies of the human condition.

The words to be quoted have again the familiar ring of the Liturgy: they appear in the epistle of the Sunday within the octave of the Nativity, and no doubt they are well known to the ordinary Catholic. It is a remarkable thing that the Church should lay such stress on our getting acquainted with the great spiritual truth of our freedom in Christ.

> But before the faith came, we were kept under the law shut up, unto that faith which was to be revealed. Wherefore the law was our pedagogue in Christ, that we might be justified by faith. But after the faith is come, we are no longer under a pedagogue. For you are all the children of God by faith in Christ Jesus. For as many of you as have been baptized in Christ have put on Christ. There is neither Jew, nor Greek: there is neither bond, nor free: there is neither male, nor female. For you are all one in Christ Jesus. And if you be Christ's, then are you the seed of Abraham, heirs according to the promise (GAL 3:23 to end).

> Now I say, as long as the heir is a child, he differeth nothing from a servant, though he be lord of all: but is under tutors and governors until the time appointed by the father: So we also, when we were children, were serving under the elements of the world. But when the fulness of the time was come, God sent his Son, made of a woman, made under the law: That he might redeem them who were under the law: that we might receive the adoption of sons. And because you are sons, God hath sent the Spirit of his Son into your hearts, crying: Abba, Father. Therefore now he is not a servant, but a son. And if a son, an heir also through God. But then indeed, not knowing God, you served them who, by nature, are not gods (GAL 4:1-8).

The third argument from the Galatians, which makes the sixth of my series, is again part of the Mass Liturgy. I need hardly do more than transcribe it. It is a well-known passage, and it embodies once more the idea of the free and gratuitous promise made to Abraham.

St. Paul, for once, stops to give the allegory a connected sequel of thought, when in the twenty-fifth verse of the fourth chapter, from which this quotation is taken, he makes Sinai, the Mount in Arabia, the parallel of the earthly Jerusalem, by reason of the geographical affinity. This sixth argument differs from the preceding ones in this, that instead of the individual soul, it is the whole new Jerusalem, the Church, that is the freewoman:

> Tell me, you that desire to be under the law, have you not read the law? For it is written that Abraham had two sons; the one by a bond-woman, and the other by a free-woman. But he who was of the bond-woman, was born according to the flesh; but of the free-woman was by promise. Which things are said by an allegory; for these are the two testaments. The one from Mount Sinai, engendering unto bondage: which is Hagar. For Sinai is a mountain in Arabia, which hath affinity to that Jerusalem which now is, and is in bondage with her children. But that Jerusalem which is above is free: which is our mother. For it is written: Rejoice, thou barren, that bearest not; break forth and cry, thou that travailest not: for many are the children of the desolate, more than of her that hath a husband. Now we, brethren, as Isaac was, are the children of promise. But as then he that was born according to the flesh persecuted him that was after the spirit: so also it is now. But what saith the scripture? Cast out the bond-woman and her son: for the son of the bond-woman shall not be heir with the son of the free-woman. So then, brethren, we are not the children of the bond-woman, but of the free: by the freedom wherewith Christ has made us free (GAL 4:21 to end).

The last argument in favor of Christ's spirituality occurs in the Epistle to the Colossians. It is less well known, and the concluding sentences only are used in the Liturgy as an Easter phraseology. In this passage we again find St. Paul at his best.

It is metaphor within metaphor, it is a playing with light and shade such as only a very poetical mind, is capable of. I shall first quote the whole section of the aforesaid epistle appertaining to my subject. I must confess that it would be necessary to transcribe the whole epistle to the Colossians, if one were to give the argument its proper setting; but nothing is easier for my reader than to take up his New Testament himself, and go through this beautiful epistle.

What St. Paul says of Christ's supereminent spiritual glories in the first chapter, and in the earlier parts of the second chapter, is all meant to lead up to his practical theme, viz. to save his converts from relapsing into lower and false forms of spirituality.

But the argument proper, where the Apostle begins to come to close grips with the enemy, may be said to start at the eighth verse of Chapter 2:

> Beware lest any man cheat you by philosophy, and vain deceit: according to the tradition of men, according to the elements of the world, and not according to Christ: For in him dwelleth all fullness of the Godhead corporally: And you are filled in him, who is the head of all principality and power: In whom also you are circumcised with circumcision not made by hand in despoiling of the body of the flesh, but in the circumcision of Christ: Buried with him in baptism, in whom also you are risen again by the faith of the operation of God, who hath raised him up from the dead. And you, when you were dead in your sins, and the uncircumcision of your flesh: he hath quickened together with him, forgiving you all offences: Blotting out the handwriting of the decree that was against us, which was contrary to us. And he hath taken the same out of the way, fastening it to the cross: And despoiling

the principalities and powers, he hath exposed them confidently in open show, triumphing over them in himself. Let no man therefore judge you in meat or in drink, or in respect of a festival day, or of the new moon, or of the sabbaths. Which are a shadow of things to come, but the body is of Christ. Let no man seduce you, willing in humility, and religion of angels, walking in the things which he hath not seen, in vain puffed up by the sense of his flesh. And not holding the head, from which the whole body, by joints and bands being supplied with nourishment and compacted, groweth unto the increase of God. If then you be dead with Christ from the elements of this world, why do you yet decree as though living in the world? Touch not, taste not, handle not; which all are unto destruction by the very use, according to the precepts and doctrines of men. Which things have indeed a show of wisdom in superstition and humility, and not sparing the body: not in any honor to the filling of the flesh (Col 2:8-23).

Therefore, if you be risen with Christ, seek the things that are above: where Christ is sitting at the right hand of God: Mind the things that are above, not the things that are upon the earth. For you are dead: and your life is hid with Christ in God. When Christ shall appear, who is your life, then you also shall appear with him in glory (Col 3:1-4).

The great liberation from the "elements of the world" as St. Paul so aptly calls everything that is lower than Christ Himself, is here expressed in five different metaphors amongst which there is one only he has already made use of.

The old circumcision itself, his *béte noire*, is turned into a thing of beauty. "You are circumcised ... in the circumcision of Christ" (Col 2:11).

Then there is the sacrament of baptism, that glorious successor of the old carnal rite. "You are buried with him in Baptism" (Col 2:12). It is the idea we found already in the Epistle to the Romans.

The third and fourth metaphors are new, and deeply original, and found nowhere else in St. Paul's writings. They speak of Christ's absolute triumph over the old order of things, and over the power that swayed the old order.

It is the metaphor of the bill that is fixed on the cross. "Blotting out the handwriting of the decree that was against us, which was contrary to us. And he hath taken the same out of the way, fastening it to the cross" (Col 2:14).

Then there is the triumphal procession, Christ leading all vanquished powers, as their captor, to the Capitol. "And despoiling the principalities and powers, he hath led them confidently in open show, triumphing over them, in himself" (Col 2:15).

There is finally the metaphor of the body versus the shadow, which is supplemented by the idea that Christ is the head. "The body is Christ's, and from the head the whole body by the joints and bands, being supplied with nourishment, and compacted, groweth into the increase of God" (Col 2:19).

With such a presentment of Christ's care, and of the soul's nearness to Him, who would still mould his mind by ancient and low standards? "Why do you yet decree as living in the world" (Col 2:20)? Let it all depart before the glory of the Easter sun; life in Christ is the only thing worth cherishing:

> Therefore if you be risen with Christ, seek the things that are above: where Christ is sitting at the right hand of God: mind the things that are above, not the things that are upon the earth. For you are dead: and your life is hid with Christ in God. When Christ shall appear, who is your life, then you also shall appear with him in glory (Col 3:1-4).

It might be said without fear of exaggeration that the whole theory of the Christian Mind is contained in the argumentations of St. Paul here set forth before the reader. St. Paul's great contention is that Christ is a heavenly substitute for all law, containing the virtue of all law in Himself, *per modum eminentiae* (by way of eminence).

All other considerations concerning the nature of the Christian Mind flow from this central thought: the Son of God, Jesus Christ, is such as to incarnate in Himself all the needs, and laws, and hopes, and destinies of man.

The following chapters of my book will be nothing else than an expansion of this root fact of the Incarnation. They will cover practically the whole subject of the Christian Mind, I mean those elements of our higher life which are derived specifically from the Incarnation, though I do not profess to set them forth in a strictly logical order. It is impossible to dissect logically a Personality, and it must always be borne in mind that the Christian Mind is a religious philosophy based on a divine Personality.

IX

The New Creature in Christ

St. Paul's concept of man's transformation through the life that comes from the Incarnation, is as radical as possible. The Incarnation is simply a new creation, and through Christ, and in Christ, we are new creatures:

> For we are his workmanship, created in Christ Jesus in good works, which God hath prepared that we should walk in them (Eph 2: 10).

> And put on the new man, who according to God is created in justice and holiness of truth (Eph 4:24).

> If then any be in Christ a new creature, the old things are passed away, behold all things are made new (2 Cor 5:17).

The Greek term κτίσις (*ktisis*) has a very definite meaning in St. Paul's writings. It stands for creation in its specific significance, as the act of God, or the product of God, implying omnipotence.

All things that are, are God's creation. When therefore St. Paul repeats with such insistence, that in Christ a new creation has taken place, he is writing in his own way something as great, and as original as the first chapter of Genesis. Man is remade, recreated in the Son of God, not with an inferior sort of κτίσις — creation — but with one that is the proper act of God, such as God exerted when He made all things at the beginning. And the new creature that is in Christ lives and thrives on that creative act of God, just as the created universe rests on the divine *fiat* that brought it out of nothingness.

Here, as in many other instances, it is merely our mental timidity that makes us attach to the words of the inspired writer a meaning different and inferior to their direct and native significance. Why should I take in a diminished and lower sense the word κτίσις — creation — when St. Paul utters it in connection with the great supernatural reality, which is our life in Christ? Why should I qualify its bearing, or modify its literalness? Surely the Incarnation and its results are not such as to give rise to hyperbole in language, as their reality will always be greater than any words contrived by man to express them. It is therefore both my right, and my privilege to give the term κτίσις in connection with the life in Christ as literal an interpretation as I do to the same word when it states the great fact that God made all things out of nothing.

To take the term "creation" in its direct and literal sense in connection with the supernatural order of things which is based on the Incarnation, leads us at once to one most precious result for our spiritual estate: through Christ we are lifted bodily above the ordinary human conditions. We are transplanted into a new world, whose laws and rules and conditions have finality and completeness in themselves. This new world is not necessarily an opposition to the first, the natural world created by God; it is above it, it has higher and more permanent rights and laws than the first, the natural creation.

To conceive Christ, and ourselves in Him, as a totally new creation with all the universal laws inherent to a creation, settles once for all a subtle perplexity of the Christian Mind; the Christian's relation with the merely natural order of things, and its legitimate interests and aspirations. How is the Christian, who is part of a new creation, to make use of the first, the old creation?

The two creations could not be at enmity, as they are both the act and the product of God. As I said, the same term κτίσις expresses the making of the world, and the making of the Christ and His graces. It is the incommunicable act of God. Therefore both creative acts, though resulting in a lower and a higher order of things, come from the same source.

The Christian, therefore, ought to be completely at home in every aspect and in every phase of creation, precisely because *qua* Christian he is God's creation, and *qua* man again he is God's creation. There is indeed in him a duality of life, the life of nature, and the life of grace. But this duality is not an opposition, as it comes from one and the same fountainhead, God's causative omnipotence:

> Every creature of God (κτίσμα) is good, and nothing to be rejected that is received with thanks giving: for it is sanctified by the word of God and prayer. These things proposing to the brethren, thou shalt be a good minister of Christ Jesus (1 Tim 4:4-7).

Such is the general principle laid down by St. Paul as to the worth and moral position of the natural creation.

Already at that early period there were signs of a false, unchristian dualism. There were "spirits of error, and doctrines of devils, speaking lies in hypocrisy, and having their conscience seared, forbidding to marry, and (wanting people) to abstain from meats" (1 Tim 4:1-4). Of such temporal solaces St. Paul affirms that "God hath created (them) to be received with thanksgiving by the faithful, and by them that have known the truth" (1 Tim 4:3).

A false, hypocritical reluctance to enter into communion with the things of the natural order, besides leading to a most disastrous spiritual pride, takes it for granted that nature is not God's creation, that there is a chasm between Christ and the natural universe. But if this inhuman dualism is healed in man through his knowledge that both nature and grace are the creation of God in him, there is the other and more important healing in his mind, through the fact that the grace of the Incarnation, being a true creation, has a superior and independent state with regard to nature.

The claims of the Incarnation on man are infinite, because the Incarnation is an infinite mystery of life. Nature however vast, is finite, with finite claims on man's allegiance. When therefore man is at any time tempted to give too much to nature, he is brought back to the golden mean through the infinitely vaster, and more persistent claims of the Incarnation.

Now St. Paul, when speaking of the grace of Christ as a new creation, exclusively has in view this aspect. The claims of the Incarnation are so great as to make all other claims appear small.

He is concerned chiefly with the claim of race and nationality. Without entering into the relative value of such claims, he simply states that in virtue of the new creation in Christ, such a perfect brotherhood, such a complete community of blood exists between Christians, that racial differences, however legitimate, are in no danger of becoming excessive, if Christian grace be given a chance:

> For in Christ Jesus neither circumcision availeth anything, nor uncircumcision, but a new creature (GAL 6:15).

> Putting on the new, (man) him who is renewed unto knowledge, according to the image of him that created him. Where there is neither Gentile nor Jew, circumcision nor uncircumcision, Barbarian nor Scythian, bond nor free. But Christ is all, in all (COL 3:10-12).

This supernatural internationalism of St. Paul, the consequence of his clear vision of the New Creation in Christ, was as bold and difficult then as it is to-day, when racial passions are so sorely on edge. Yet this attitude of the Christian Mind is the only saving element that can redeem the nations from the absurd and appalling results of racialism out of bounds. For a good many centuries already Christian thought and national thought have been happily wedded together. The most unworldly follower of Christ is a lover of his country. It is the practical realization of St. Paul's utterance that all creature is good.

Periodically the question is put to Catholics, whether their religion or their allegiance to their respective country holds the first place in their minds. Non-Catholics seem to think that in the minds of the perfect Christian there is such a dualism, when in fact it is nowhere to be found.

One might as well ask a chance citizen of any state what holds the first place in his mind, whether it is personal honesty, or loyalty to this country. He would be puzzled no doubt by such a division of his own person. For him honesty and loyalty to a State are inseparable things. But, on second thoughts, he might find out that loyalty is contained in personal honesty, as a smaller thing may be contained in a bigger thing. Personal honesty is something more universal, as all men may possess personal honesty, whilst loyalty to a definite community of men and interests is only possible then, when such a community exists.

After all it is at least theoretically possible for men to live without such definite, sharply divided communities, whilst personal honesty is at the base of all human life that is superior to animal instincts. Personal honesty can never be truly in opposition to any legitimate loyalty, as no sound cause can be served by anything that is not honesty. Therefore it is as idle as it is irritating to ask a man such questions. Enough for him to know that patriotism is part of general virtuousness, though it be not all virtuousness.

So likewise with that new creation, the Christian Mind. The all-embracing charity of Christ is the greater, the more universal thing. Any other love, as love of one's country, is the smaller thing, contained in the great universal, the charity of Christ. To ask which is first, and which is second in our hearts, Christ or the nation to which we belong, is as silly a question as if I addressed myself to the man in the street, puzzling him with the poser, whether he wants to be an Englishman first, and then an honest man, or vice versa.

All things are the creation of God, but Christ holds in all things the "primacy" (COL 1:18). All things are in Him and under Him and therefore all things are lovable. Nothing that is true and good need ever be sacrificed on the altar of Christ, it merely needs to be brought into subjection to Him, into line and harmony with His own lovableness. This universality of charity that recognizes no difference of races in the higher sphere where Christ dwells, is perfectly compatible with difference of special claims on the part of the one nation to which we belong.

But it is not compatible with any kind of hatred, except the hatred of iniquity. Patriotism is no more served by racial hatred than it is by dishonesty. It simply renders man unfit for that immense human advantage of entering into communion with the wealth, spiritual and material, of other nations. A nation is immensely the poorer if through blind hatred it renders itself unfit for such a participation in the good things of the human race. Its blindness brings its own castigation at once.

The new creature in Christ is therefore the finest mental attitude for all genuine diplomacy. No men are more fit to handle the great international difficulties than the men who love all races in Christ, and before whose mind the infinitely great factor of universal Redemption through the Incarnation stands out as the one unchanging institution. The Christian Mind, in virtue of the grace of the new Creation, is endowed with the truest and soundest kind of internationalism, besides having its own legitimate preferences. A thousand wars, lost or won, cannot do away with the claims of the new Creation in Christ.

We Christians simply must love all men in Christ. If we refuse to do so, we can have no share in the new Creation. Nationalism in religion makes of nationalism itself a most unreasonable thing, a thing charged with most dangerous potentialities. Les us rejoice and glory in our new Creation in Christ, and all creation will be our home.

The boldest statement of this spiritual superiority to racial exclusiveness is found in St. Paul's Second Epistle to the Corinthians:

> Wherefore henceforth, we know no man according to the flesh …
> And if we have known Christ according to the flesh: but now we know him so no longer (2 Cor 5:16).

Christ the Messiah was more than anything else the boast of the Jewish nation, by anticipation. The Messiah to their minds was essentially Jewish.

His mission according to their belief would be a great racial mission. Such had been the dream of Saul of Tarsus. He too, before being struck down by the light from Heaven, was all aglow with hope and fervor for a national Messiah. It was an enthusiasm all according to the flesh.

But when Christ, the Son of David, manifested Himself finally to the mental eyes of Saul, in His own transcending glory, then Saul understood the mystery of Christ's glorious universalism. At once he felt lifted up to a new world, the limits of which are infinitude itself. And this new world is Christ's.

Paul can move freely in it, his mind travels over it without check or hindrance. In an ecstasy of joy he cries out:

> If then any (man) be in Christ, (he is) a new creature; the old things are passed away, behold all things are made new (2 Cor 5:17).

X

The Central Attitude of the Christian Mind

Spiritual tendencies are often represented as being either centripetal, or centrifugal. This division, taken from natural science, is an easily understood simile. Centripetal tendencies are movements of the mind towards the center of all things, God; centrifugal tendencies are the opposite: they are the tendencies that are destructive of the harmony and unity in things spiritual. It goes without saying that the Christian Mind is radically centripetal: all its tendencies and aspirations are towards God, and they make for harmony and unity.

The obedience of the Christian Mind is at bottom nothing else than this blissful convergence of all its powers towards the eternal center of all light and truth, God.

But there is something more in the Christian Mind than this centripetal tendency. The Christian Mind not only tends towards the great center, God, but it is *central*, not only centripetal. It occupies a central position from the very start. It is in Christ in a most excellent way, and from that great center, Christ, it looks at all things.

The peace of God, which surpasseth all understanding, keep your hearts and minds in Christ Jesus (Phil 4:7).

As God is in Christ, reconciling the world unto Himself, so, on a finite and analogous scale, the perfectly educated mind in the things of the Incarnation is in Christ, as in its natural center, looking at the world from that sublime height, and bringing all things into convergent lines in virtue of that central position. It is quite evident that the early Christian Mind was thus centered in Christ.

To the faithful of the first Christian period there only was one great object for mental contemplation, the Son of God in His power and glory. They looked at the world in general, and at mankind in particular, through the Son of God, I might almost say, from the height of Christ's glory. To them mankind was practically an indifferent thing, incapable of arousing interest. Their interest was centered on Christ, and His grace; the propagation of that grace, the preaching of the name of Christ, for its own sake, because it is the greatest of all names, such were their aspirations.

Their missionary zeal was more love of Christ, than love of mankind. They knew nothing about mankind, they only dreaded its dark enmities. But they knew much about Christ, and they basked in the sunshine of His love. They were sure of Him. In fact He was their only security, their true harbor of refuge.

In Him alone they dared to approach the world. If their preaching was successful, it was Christ's power operating through them. If their mission failed, it was Christ's judgment on an unworthy world. As for themselves, neither failure nor success could alter their sense of spiritual possession. They possessed Christ, and in Him they possessed Heaven and earth, whatever the attitude of their fellow-men.

That such was practically the primitive Christian attitude of mind, and above all of the attitude of St. Paul, can be proved by innumerable references. In order to understand such an attitude more clearly, let us compare it with another attitude of mind, extremely common in our days amongst those who have the missionary spirit.

In our time, most people look at mankind first. It is their paramount interest. They love it, and pity it for its own sake. In consequence, if they are fervent Christians, they are anxious to see as many men and women converted to Christ as possible. If believers are few, they feel as if they belonged spiritually to a small world only. There is a general sentiment of disappointment in their life. If on the contrary, believers are many, their heart is dilated with the satisfaction of being the children of a great Kingdom. Their first and leading thought is the conversion of mankind, not the coming of Christ.

Humanity, its evolution and its progress are the fetishes of modern non-Christian thought. Everywhere we find the religion of humanity pushing back the worship of the Son of God. It is the sort of religion that becomes easily popular, as it has all the external signs of love and philanthropy. In a certain way, this idea of the predominant value of humanity has affected Christian thought. Mankind is the most assertive thing for the minds of many believers, and the conditions of salvation for mankind as a whole are more absorbing and perplexing problems to them than they were to other generations of Christians.

As in many other instances of subordinate truths, the minor truth is a helpful and salutary attitude of the mind, so long as it is regulated by the greater truth. Taken away from the control of the vaster verity, the lesser truth easily becomes an aberration, a mental disturbance. So in this matter of the relative importance of mankind and Christ. To love mankind is a good thing; to love it outside Christ gives it at once a disproportionate place in the mind. To give to mankind any other place but a subordinate one, would be a great mental disorder in those who believe in the Son of God: for them the one Son of God made man is an infinitely vaster thing than the whole aggregate of men, past, present, and future.

The great questions for the Christian Mind are all the questions that have the Son of God directly for their object. What is He in Himself, and what are His dealings with the children of men? This is what I call the central attitude of the Christian Mind.

Nowhere in the Gospels do we hear Christ giving utterance to a hope that mankind as such, as the human race, will ever be conquered by His grace in this world, will ever believe in Him and love Him. On the contrary, He solemnly describes Himself as being accessible only to certain preordained classes of people:

> At that time Jesus answered and said: I confess to thee, O Father, Lord of Heaven and earth, because thou hast hid these things from the wise and prudent, and hast revealed them to little ones. Yea, Father: for so hath it seemed good in thy sight. All things are delivered to me by my Father. And no one knoweth the Son, but the Father: neither doth any one know the Father, but the Son, and he to whom it shall please the Son to reveal him (MATT. 11:25-27).

Of universal and uncontested conquest of mankind to the obedience of His faith, there is never any hope in the mind and on the lips of Christ. On the contrary, His forebodings are of the gloomiest:

> Will not God revenge his elect who cry to him day and night: and will he have patience in their regard? I say to you that he will quickly revenge them. But yet the Son of man when he cometh, shall he find, think you, faith on earth (LUKE 18:7-8).

With constant utterance as to the universality of His power, our Lord couples assertions not less emphatic as to the limited number of His followers, and the restricted success of the Gospel. His disciples are bidden to look upon mankind generally as upon a hostile, savage power:

> Behold I send you as sheep in the midst of wolves. Be ye therefore wise as serpents, and simple as doves. But beware of men (MATT 10:16-17).

On the other hand, they are bidden to meet the world covered with their faith in the Son of God, as with armor. To go out to the world in their own name, and in their own wisdom, would be suicidal to them.

But when they shall deliver you up, take no thought how or what to speak: for it shall be given you in that hour what to speak. For it is not you that speak, but the Spirit of your Father that speaketh in you (Matt 10:19-20).

Nothing would be easier than to accumulate quotations from St. Paul showing how he possessed that central attitude of mind, how to him Apostolic activity was essentially a glorification of Christ, and how he practically ignored all things outside Christ:

What have I to do to judge them that are without? ... For them that are without, God will judge (1 Cor 5:12-13).

"Without" here means outside Christ's faith.

There is in St. Paul a marked love for the predestination view of things, taking the word here in its true orthodox sense. He knows Christ and those that are in Christ; he is full of activity, travels all over the world to convert to Christ those that are predestined to Christ's grace, whose election has made them already to be Christ's potentially. Outside that Christ circle, he has no real interest. Whatever is beyond it, he leaves to the judgment of God; it is no concern of his. The spiritual destinies of that "without" are not even a problem to his mind. It is no part of his world.

That such is the attitude of St Paul's mind is beyond doubt. Christ and the things of Christ are essentially life, a practical activity of the heart and the mind. Outside Christ, nothing is practical, nothing is feasible or possible in the spiritual order of things. So there is practically for St. Paul's mind only one sphere of things, the sphere of which Christ is the center.

Now and then it would seem as if the great Apostle were concerned with the questions of more universal salvation, in a less concentric frame of mind. In the second chapter to the Romans he alludes to the possibility of spiritual justification for the Gentiles to whom no Revelation has been granted, and who "show the work of the law written in their hearts, their conscience bearing witness to them" (Rom 2:15). In 1 Tim 2:3-4, he says of "God our Savior" that "He will have all men to be saved, and to come to the knowledge of the truth". Again in, 1 Tim 4:10, God is said to be "the Savior of all men, especially of the faithful."

Better known still are St. Paul's pathetic utterances concerning the salvation of the Jewish people who had not believed in Christ:

> Brethren, the will of my heart, indeed, and my prayer to God is, for them unto salvation (ROM 10:1).

But in all these utterances St. Paul's mind never leaves its center. The salvation which God has in store for us all, the prayer of St. Paul, the judgment over the heathen who has not known the Law, it is all in Christ. The heathen's conscience will be his accuser or defender "in the day when God shall judge the secrets of men by Jesus Christ, according to my Gospel" (ROM 2:16).

In the Gospel of St. John this divine "centralness" is most evident:

> All things were made by him: and without him was made nothing that was made. In him was life, and the life was the light of men (JOHN 3:4).

All through St. John's Gospel we find the exclusiveness of the infinite stated most emphatically. Christ is infinite life, yet it is an infinitude to which only a few have access, which practically touches only a chosen number. The failure of Christ's mission with regard to individuals is one of the facts most insisted upon in St. John's Gospel:

> Remember my word that I said to you: The servant is not greater than his master. If they have persecuted me, they will also persecute you; if they have kept my word, they will keep yours also (JOHN 15:20).

But with all this failure, the great life, the great kingdom of God is in no way damaged, or circumscribed. It is all fullness from the very beginning, and those that believe are beyond the reach of disappointment:

That which my Father hath given me, is greater than all: and no one can snatch them out of the hand of my Father (JOHN 10:29).

Even then, when St. Paul uses expressions that might at first sight denote more universal aspirations, his universalisms never go outside Christ. It is St. Paul's dream to present every man perfect, not simply without qualifications, but in Christ Jesus, in Whom also he labors, as if He were the proper field of his activities, and as if all his movements were contained within His infinitude of grace:

> To whom (i.e. the Saints) God would make known the riches of the glory of this mystery among the Gentiles, which is Christ, in you the hope of glory. Whom we preach, admonishing every man, and teaching every man in all wisdom, that we may present every man perfect in Christ Jesus, wherein also I labour, striving according to his working which he worketh in me in power (COL 1:27-30).

XI

Our Equality in Christ

The inequalities of human life and human conditions have been a trial to man's patience at all times. Certain generations have felt them more than others: but no time has been without the angry rumblings of man's resentment at the inequalities of human destinies. From the revolt of slaves and plebeians in the Roman world, to the idolization of equality in the French revolution, it may be a far cry in point of time; in point of psychology it is the same threatening voice of offended humanity.

To the practical theories of human equality which are at the root of the socialism of all times, there corresponds in the realm of thought a distinct socialism of outlook. Many philosophical and even religious systems are to a great extent the outcome of unconscious rebellion against privilege and preference, either in the order of nature or even in the Christian dispensation.

It was to be expected that the problem of human inequalities should be brought into contact with the grace of the Incarnation, and if a solution were possible, that it should be solved in Christ. It is very gratifying, then, to see this problem constantly brought up by St. Paul, and as constantly solved in the same manner.

The mind of the Apostle had grasped the principle from the very beginning, and he applies it with perfect appropriateness and success to the most diverse cases. The principle is one of the most precious elements of the Christian Mind, and it is as original as the Eucharist, or the *Pleroma* (fullness), with which in fact this principle of equality is intimately associated. It comes to this: Christ is substantive fullness. As such, He fills up all inequalities, so that he who is less, or has less, provided he be in Christ, is not really unequal to him that is more, or has more. Such is, to my thinking, the general enunciation of the principle of equality in Christ. Whilst safeguarding the difference of attribute and gifts, it does away with inequality of condition:

> He that had much, had nothing over: and he that had little, had no want (2 COR 8:15).

We must make a distinction between difference of gifts, nay, even inequalities of gifts, and inequalities of condition. Gifts in the natural and spiritual order may differ; there may be more or less of them; they may even be called unequal gifts, but such scales of more and less, so long as they do not produce inequalities of condition of existence, are not resented by man. But the moment the higher endowment isolates its possessor from the man less endowed, makes of him a being apart, the difference is resented, the inequality is no longer in the gift, but in the mode of existence.

Wealth is the main object of human jealousies, not so much on account of the greater physical enjoyments it brings with itself, as on account of the gulf there is between the wealthy and the poor, socially. Wherever Christian charity bridges over the gulf, when the true fraternity between rich and poor is a practical fact of life, it is wonderful how little resentment there is on the part of the more destitute classes against the rich.

The Son of God in His own person has abolished all inequalities of conditions, in things spiritual and natural, in Heaven and on earth, though there be in Him diversity of gifts and grace and ministries, though there be in Him the more excellent and the less excellent way: and it is one of the greatest privileges of the Christian Mind to have grasped this divine fact.

This wonderful achievement of the Son of God is tersely put by St. Paul in the Epistle to the Ephesians.

> But to every one of us is given grace according to the measure of the giving of Christ. Wherefore he saith: Ascending on high, he led captivity captive, he gave gifts to men. Now that he ascended, what is it, but because he also descended first into the lower parts of the earth? He that descended is the same also that ascended above all the heavens, that he might fill all things (Eph 4:7-11).

There is no region in the Father's creation which the Incarnate Son does not fill with the presence of His power. And this all-pervading presence of the Son of God, this prior occupation by Him of all things, makes it impossible for any power to bring about a real inequality of conditions in those that possess such power. There may be more power in some, less power in others: but there can be no real inequality, in the condition of existence amongst creatures that live, and move, and have their being in a world whose most distant regions and sections are filled with the presence of the Son of God.

And what is true of the gifts, is likewise true of the more static element, sanctity, in its specific meaning. There is the greater sanctity, and the lesser sanctity, amongst the elect: there are the higher spirits, and there are the lower spirits. But as Christ is the head of all, as His grace is in them all, the element of union in Him infinitely outweighs the element of variety in the degrees of grace and glory:

> And he (God) hath subjected all things under his feet, and hath made him head over all the church. Which his is body, and the fullness of him who is filled all in all (Eph 1:22-23).

The practical conclusions of this great principle are not far to seek, and St. Paul points them out most clearly. There is in fact hardly anything more completely worked out by the great Apostle, if we except his teaching about law and grace, than this principle of Christ's unifying role as the God-Man.

It is the thought that underlies St. Paul's divine metaphor of the Body of Christ, and its mutualities of service and sympathy. The old parable or Agrippa, who succeeded in soothing the Roman plebs in their rebellions against social inequalities, has been given by St. Paul an extension and a meaning that stretches into the infinite. Here again the reader will forgive the full recital of the Pauline texts:

> For as the body is one, and hath many members: and all the members of the body, whereas they are many, yet are one body, so also is Christ. For in one Spirit were we all baptized into one body, whether Jews or Gentiles, whether bond or free; and in one Spirit we have all been made to drink. For the body also is not one member, but many. If the foot should say, because I am not the hand, I am not of the body; is it therefore not of the body? And if the ear should say, because I am not the eye, I am not of the body; is it therefore not of the body? If the whole body were the eye: where would be the hearing? If the whole were hearing: where would be the smelling? But now God hath set the members every one of them in the body as it hath pleased Him. And if they were one member, where would be the body? But now there are many members indeed, yet one body. And the eye cannot say to the hand: I need not thy help; nor again the head to the feet: I have no need of you. Yea, much more those that seem to be the more feeble members of the body, are more necessary. And such as we think to be the less honourable members of the body, about these we put more abundant honor; and those that are our uncomely parts, have more abundant comeliness. But our comely parts have no need: but God hath tempered the body together, giving to that which wanted the more abundant honor. That there might be no schism in the body, but the members might be mutually careful one for another. And if one member suffer anything, all the members suffer with it, or if one member glory, all the members rejoice with it. Now you are the body of

Christ, and members of member. And God indeed hath set some in the Church, first apostles, secondly prophets, thirdly doctors; after that miracles, then the graces of healings, helps, governments, kinds of tongues, interpretations of speeches (1 Cor 12:12-28).

XII

THE CHRISTIAN MIND AND ETERNAL LIFE

To expect eternal life for the just, and as a reward of sanctity, belongs to the general Christian mind.

All religious men of all ages have hoped for a happy and never ending existence beyond the grave. Their efforts at representing the nature of that life have met with varying success. Some men have seen more clearly than others what immortality of soul means for the just; but all good men have believed in the fundamental fact of immortality.

The Catholic doctrine of Beatific Vision is certainly the loftiest, as well as the truest expression of the state of the elect in the world to come. It is a doctrine that has been worked out as completely as human intellect can do it by the Christian Theologians. Yet glorious as it is, and sublime as it is, and though it was never grasped clearly except amongst Christians, I should not class it amongst the doctrines that are specifically Christian, as depending intrinsically on the doctrine of Incarnation. For there could be Beatific Vision even if God had not taken to Himself a human nature.

The argument and ground on which the holy men of all times have based their hopes for a blessed immortality also belong to the general Christian mind. Such arguments and motives of belief are partly inherent in our reasoning natures, and partly they are God's revelation. But they have no distinct connection with the fact that God became Incarnate. Yet nothing could be more false than the conviction that the Incarnation has not brought us an entirely new set of views and doctrines and arguments, with regard to the great question of the fate of the just who live and die in the grace of Christ.

As there is the general Christian doctrine of eternal life, the specific Christian Mind moves in spheres unknown to the general Christian mind, when it thinks of man's Hereafter. Christ's resurrection and ascension into Heaven constitute for the Christian Mind a ground of hope quite different from all other reasons of hoping, and the eternal life of the faithful Christian is a necessary concomitant of the glorious estate of the risen Christ.

Eternal life for the specific Christian Mind is essentially life in Christ, and life with Christ, a condition of existence that includes all other facts known to man about his own personal survivance. When he wants to have an irrefragable proof of the reality of eternal life for the just, the Christian turns for arguments not to philosophy, nor to the traditions of mankind, but he goes directly to Christ's sepulcher. Christ is risen, and He will not die again, and this glorious fact settles forever all his hesitations and perplexities. He knows that there is such a thing as eternal life for man.

He may be well instructed in philosophy; he may be capable of reasoning out the logical necessity of immortality for man's spirit; he may be deeply impressed by the fact that all human goodness has always lived on the conviction that there is the great Hereafter; he may live on the generic Christian faith of retribution for the good in the land of the living. But all such supports and props to his mind hardly appear. His mind is suffused with the glory of Christ's resurrection, and eternal life is merely the radiance of the risen Son of God.

Christians ought to dread nothing more than a diminution of their faith in Christ's bodily resurrection, as such a -diminution would be the loss of our chief and most congenial ground for belief in our own personal immortality. For as Christians, and in virtue of our mystical incorporation with the Incarnate God, all our future hopes are based on Christ's resurrection.

Once more I say that we do not ignore other motives for holding the belief in man's survival after death; nowhere are such motives searched into, and probed, and held with greater reverence than in Catholic schools of thought. Yet when all has been said, the mental satisfaction derived from such meditations is as nothing, when compared with the overpowering conviction that there is eternal life for us, which comes to us from the constant contemplation of the sweet mystery of Easter.

To speak and think lightly of the mystery of Christ's bodily rising from the dead, and to cling keenly to the merely philosophical grounds of belief in our soul's immortality is indeed to sell our birthright for the pottage of lentils. I do not enter here into the question whether it is possible for the human reason, in the long run, to hold logically, and as a deliberate conviction, any doctrines as to man's personal immortality, and reject at the same as an impossibility the dogma of Christ's resurrection.

I do not believe that faith in man's personal survival after death could have deep roots in a mind that recoils from the faith in Christ's resurrection. All I need say here is that the doctrine of Christ's resurrection being a specifically Christian doctrine is of such a nature as to give us an unshakable assurance of our personal immortality: so that for us temptations of doubt and despair are best overcome, not so much by investigations into the philosophical grounds of the soul's immortality, as by meditating humbly on the sweet mystery of our Lord's resurrection.

Such is evidently St. Paul's mental attitude with regard to the motives why we should look forward, each of us, to a happy immortality. The resurrection of Christ establishes forever the fact that the dead, at least those that died in Christ, will also rise. A happy eternity in the mind of St. Paul is identical with fellowship in Christ's resurrection:

> For if we believe that Jesus died, and rose again, even so them who have slept through Jesus will God bring with him (1 THESS 4:13).

The powerful reasoning of St. Paul in the fifteenth chapter of his first Epistle to the Corinthians establishes the general truth, that there is a resurrection awaiting Christ's disciples, on the fact that Christ rose from the dead, Who is "the first fruits of them that sleep" (1 Cor 15:20).

St. Paul's mind at first sight seems to move in a way that is the inversion of the movements of the ordinary logical mind. The ordinary logical mind would deduce the fact of one individual being's resurrection from the general truth that there is a resurrection whilst St. Paul deduces the general truth of universal resurrection from the particular fact that Christ rose.

But the inversion is merely apparent. As Christ's resurrection is the cause of all other resurrections, it is really something vaster, something more general and more universal than the general truth of the resurrection of all the just:

> For by a man came death, and by a man the resurrection of the dead. And as in Adam all die, so also in Christ all shall be made alive (1 Cor 15:21-22).

There is no question as to St. Paul's mental outlook. For him, eternal life and eternal happiness simply mean participation in Christ's resurrection:

> That I may know him, and the power of his resurrection (Phil 3:10).

Several doubts might occur to the reader, when he is told that for the specific Christian Mind, the whole question of the world to come resolves itself into a keen realization of the mystery of Christ's resurrection. It might be argued that the doctrine of our Lord's resurrection with its effects on our own happy immortality, leaves entirely untouched the general question whether the souls of all men, good or bad, are immortal. Christ's resurrection, in the mind of St. Paul, seems to have a direct bearing only on the fate of the elect.

To this I answer, that the Christian Mind is not merely a speculative turn of thought, but is essentially a practical view of each one's spiritual interests. As the eternal loss of the reprobate has nothing to do with me practically, I am fully justified in reading the great question of my own eternal future in the light of Christ's resurrection, as my own future is entirely decided, and shaped by it, and by nothing else. Whether the doctrine of Christ's resurrection settles all the eschatological questions of mankind, is a point that need not be discussed here. It certainly can solve all such questions as far as they have reference to me.

Then it might be said that the doctrine of Christ's resurrection is more a doctrine for the body, than for the soul. It does not directly encourage the belief that man's soul is immortal through its own innate elements.

To this I reply, that Christ's resurrection implies all and every one of the conclusions of human philosophy and of the consensus of mankind as well as the facts of the broader Revelation to man with regard to the nature of our immortal souls. Resurrection means the survival of the soul after death, as well as the quickening of the body. The power, and the life, and the self-consciousness of Christ's soul, after the death on the cross, constituted one of the great Christian dogmas, the descent into the lower world of the just spirits, with its illuminating and saving power for the souls detained in the expectancy of the Redemption:

> Because Christ also died once for our sins, the just for the unjust: that he might offer us to God, being put to death indeed in the flesh, but enlivened in the spirit. In which also coming he preached to those spirits that were in prison: Which had been some time incredulous, when they waited for the patience of God in the days of Noah, when the ark was a building: wherein a few, that is, eight souls, were saved by water (1 PET 3:18-21).

The departure of Christ's soul from the body, its self-conscious existence, its power of enlightenment, its return to the body are all part of the resurrection mystery. No man could believe in Christ's resurrection without his apprehending most clearly the natural immortality of the human soul.

It would seem lastly, that faith in Christ's Resurrection does not of necessity imply a revelation of the more spiritual factors of eternal life, such as the clear vision of God; it would seem as if the resurrection were of the secondary order of spiritual realities, it being directly the glorification of the body, not of the soul. So it would seem as if Christ's resurrection could not be to us the glorious summary of all our hopes.

Such is the objection, and common as it is, it reveals a very great ignorance of the conditions and glories of our new life in Christ. If anything is clear, it is the fact that the bodily resurrection of Christ, and our bodily resurrection, in Him, is eternal life to the mind of St. Paul. It means the totality of our hopes, not only the possession of a secondary happiness.

Resurrection, in Apostolic language, is everything, glory of the soul, and glory of the body, triumph over the world, and vision of God. The above quotation from St. Peter's Epistle is followed by a very clear statement as to the universality of glories implied in this one thing, Christ's resurrection:

> Whereunto baptism being of the like form, now saveth you also: not the putting away of the filth of the flesh, but the examination of a good conscience towards God by the resurrection of Jesus Christ. Who is on the right hand of God, swallowing down death, that we might be made heirs of life everlasting: being gone into Heaven, the angels and powers and virtues being made subject to him (1 PET 3:21-22).

Christ Himself quite plainly identifies the mystery of man's resurrection on the last day with the mystery of man's adoption as God's child:

> And Jesus said to them: The children of this world marry, and are given in marriage: But they that shall be accounted worthy of that world and of the resurrection from the dead, shall neither be married, nor take wives. ... Neither can they die any more: for they are equal to the angels and are the children of God, being the children of the resurrection (LUKE 20:34-36).

If anything is certain, it is the fact that in the New Testament language the idea of resurrection as applied to Christ and to His elect, though it be primarily the mystery of the quickening of the body, is not a secondary spiritual factor, but is the main factor, of our glorious Hereafter.

Eternal life is simply stated as being the resurrection from the dead. It is said sometimes that through the resurrection, both in the case of Christ and His elect, a merely accidental joy and glory accrues to the human nature. Such language is hardly scriptural. Everywhere the mystery of the resurrection is spoken of as the great crowning of God's works in the natural and supernatural order, an act of God that brings with itself every other glory, every fullness of divine life:

> Now if we be dead with Christ, we believe that we shall live also together with Christ: Knowing that Christ rising again from the dead, dieth now no more, death shall no more have dominion over him. For in that he died to sin, he died once; but in that he liveth, he liveth unto God (Rom 6:8-10).

This then, is the essentially Christian attitude of mind with regard to our future life: a keen love, and a profound grasp of the great dogma of Christ's resurrection. It gives wonderful definiteness to all our hopes and aspirations. It makes of the Son of God the end of all our longings, and never the means towards something outside the Son of God, however lofty that something may be.

Our eternity is merely the participation in Christ's risen life. No words could be a better conclusion to these considerations than Christ's own confident and unequivocal assertion, in His last prayer:

> Father, I will that where I am, they also whom thou hast given me may be with me: that they may see my glory which thou hast given me, because thou hast loved me before the creation of the world (John 17:24).

Christ's eternal glory could not be put in more forcible terms. There is only one further remark before drawing this chapter to a close. The doctrine of Christ's bodily resurrection, and consequently the doctrine of our own bodily resurrection, means infinitely more than we commonly imagine. It means the complete glorification of human nature, in soul and body.

Catholic theology knows well how to distinguish between final glorification and other states of sanctity and happiness. Thus our Lord on earth had Beatific Vision, and yet, before the hour of His resurrection, He was not a glorified being, and did not enjoy the supereminent happiness of a glorified being.

On the other hand, the Saints whose souls are in Heaven now, before the great waking up of the last resurrection comes, have Beatific Vision and happiness. But it could not be said that they are in a state of glorification. Such a state will become theirs on that great day, and what they possess now is a partial anticipation of it.

These considerations ought to help us to understand better why the resurrection is, after all, the one idea that ought to stand for eternal life in minds well educated in the mystery of Christ.

XIII

THE CHRISTIAN MIND AND DEATH

Nothing in all the happenings of this world is more capable of giving rise to a greater variety of philosophies, than the ever recurring and unavoidable event of man's death. Death has been envisaged by man from the most various angles of mental perspective. It has provided the optimist and the pessimist with plenty of food for their respective mental attitudes. Both the spiritualist and the materialist have made of death the corner-stone of their theories as to the real worth and value of human things.

But coming at once to the strictly religious attitude of men towards death, we find that the dire reality of man's ending has impressed the children of men in ways that are most varied, though they are seldom, if ever, contradictory.

The physical terrors of death, the sudden snapping asunder of all the interests of life, the uncertainty of one's individual fate in the great Beyond, the fear of God's judgments, the ending of all our human activities, and many other such considerations have made of death a source of sadness even for Christians, though it be a salutary sadness. Death makes us "sorrowful according to God".

Such considerations belong of course to the general Christian mentality; the Incarnation presupposes them, and our Lord Himself made use of them in His Gospel, witness the parable of the foolish rich man, whose fields had yielded a plentiful harvest, and who had said to his soul:

> Soul, thou hast much goods laid up for many years, take thy rest, eat, drink, make good cheer (Luke 12:19).

Christ's description of that foolish man's fate is extremely striking:

> But God said to him: thou fool, this night do they require thy soul of thee, and whose shall those things be which thou hast provided (Luke 12:20).

Yet who would dare to think that the Incarnation has not lifted the philosophy of death to a much higher plane? St. Paul in the Epistle to the Hebrews asserts that a new attitude of man towards death is one of the primary results of the Incarnation:

> Therefore because the children are partakers of flesh and blood, he also himself in like manner hath been partaker of the same: that through death he might destroy him who had the empire of death, that is to say, the devil: and might deliver them, who through the fear of death were all their lifetime subject to servitude (Heb 2:14-15).

It may be stated as a broad proposition that the Incarnation has heightened the reality of all the spiritual factors of the general Christian mind, whilst in the case of death it lessens those same general factors. It lessens the terror of death, physical and spiritual; it lessens its uncertainties, its results. For as the doctrine of the resurrection of all flesh is a specifically Christian doctrine, death loses its sting through the Incarnation:

> O death, where is thy victory? O death, where is thy sting (1 Cor 14:55)?

The fact that Christ died ought to reconcile all of us to the prospect of death. A preacher who would put death before the eyes of the faithful merely as a naked reality of terror, bodily and spiritual, without softening his presentment with the sweet lights that come from the Son of God, Who tasted death in His own body, instead of building up, would merely destroy souls. His terrors would be of the lowest order, with nothing essentially Christian.

But the Incarnation has done more than merely soften the horrors of death. Not only has it overcome death, and robbed it of its sting, but it has actually abolished the difference between life and death. It has given to death the same spiritual value as to life. It has made, for those who share actively the grace of the Incarnation, life and death to be one continuous, uninterrupted function of Christ's life in man.

It is St. Paul who gives us this high and specifically Christian view of death. In his Epistle to the Romans, referring to of an apparently small matter, he soars all at once to that wonderful height of Christian thinking where life and death become confounded in the higher reality of our membership with Christ.

The occasion for so glorious a pronouncement was the settlement of a practical difficulty amongst the early Christians. To what extent were the faithful allowed to eat of the meat that had been sacrificed to the idols in the pagan temples, and was being retailed in the shops of the city butchers? St. Paul wants absolute freedom for everyone, as the meat could not be considered to have been made sacrilegious through the circumstance of having been offered to the idols. For idols are nothing, and therefore could not be said to leave a curse on the meat. Let every Christian use his own discretion, and consult his own conscience, and act in a way he thinks best calculated to give glory to the Lord.

> And he that eateth, eateth to the Lord: for he giveth thanks to God. And he that eateth not, to the Lord he eateth not, and giveth thanks to God (Rom 14:6).

But in St. Paul's mind there was present then a much larger principle, which no doubt was a constant mental habit to him. For nothing shows better to what an extent a man has assimilated a comprehensive truth than the spontaneous ease with which he applies it to the facts and perplexities of the life of every-day:

> For none of us liveth to himself: and no man dieth to himself. For whether we live, we live unto the Lord: or whether we die, we die unto the Lord. Therefore, whether we live, or whether we die, we are the Lord's. For to this end Christ died and rose again: that he might be Lord both of the dead and of the living (ROM 14:7-9).

I feel confident that my reader will easily perceive the wonderful novelty, as well as the deep significance of this view of St. Paul about life and death and their respective values. Nothing of the kind has been said by man before. In fact, how could man view life and death as mere functions of a higher life, as St. Paul does here, unless man believed that the Son of God had died and had risen from the dead, that He might be Lord both of the dead and of the living.

Now such a belief is of course a specifically Christian doctrine, and therefore I am right in saying that the view of life and death set forth here by St. Paul is absolutely original, belongs to the specific Christian Mind, and is also the highest mental attitude to which man may rise when he ponders over the problem of death.

It might be said that St. Paul's doctrine about life and death is already included in that other gracious outcome of the Incarnation, the radical identity of human conditions in Christ, of which I have spoken already. In Christ the rich are poor and the poor are rich, or, even more truly, both the rich and the poor of this world are rich in Him. Christ is all things in all. So with life and death. To be dead is not a disadvantage, because we are dead in order to live for Him: and if we are still alive, our life is not ours, but His.

Yet there is a peculiar originality of thought in St. Paul's expression that no Christian dies to himself, and that we who die, die unto the Lord, which invites further meditation. It is a comparatively easy concept that a Christian is not meant to live to himself, but unto the Lord. A Christian's life ought to be entirely dedicated to Christ: life's activities ought to have that peculiar unselfishness which comes from our having been bought at a great price, the blood of the Son of God. We are not our own, but His, and all we are and do ought to be impregnated with the purpose of glorifying Him.

But it is not so obvious a thought that is expressed in the second half of St. Paul's aphorism, that "no man dieth to himself" and that "whether we die, we die unto the Lord". The phrase would be more than clear, if it were a question of laying down one's life for Christ's name, through martyrdom. But evidently St. Paul spoke his great words irrespective of the glory of being Christ's witness in one's blood.

St. Paul speaks of the ordinary natural death of the Christian. If death then were the total cessation of man's higher life, St. Paul's phrase would be meaningless. For a cessation of all activity could not be something good, that is unto the Lord; St. Paul's words essentially imply that death, as well as life, is a gift of man to Christ his Redeemer.

Now a pure cessation and negation could never be a gift. We have to conclude therefore that the Apostle's words imply a continuation of activity, a survival of something very positive. The state of death is only another phase of our spiritual incorporation in Christ. His death was the most positive, the most spiritual thing. The Christian's death is a membership in that most adorable mystery, Christ's death. Therefore, life and death for the Christian are merely two phases of the same glorious event, our life in Christ, embracing both the state of the living and the state of death.

I say it once more, such a mental attitude is of unsurpassable beauty and truth, and its originality is as great as its beauty. Such an attitude of mind is not possible outside the grace of the Incarnation. St. Paul corroborates his view on death with the statement that "for this end Christ died and rose again, that he might be Lord both of the dead and the living". This clearly supports my contention that St. Paul considers the state of death as another phase of life. Christ's dominion over the dead is a dominion of graciousness over positive, living, conscious beings, as much as

His dominion over the living, not a -power over vague shadows, or distant memories, or unconscious personalities.

The Son of God in St. John's Revelation gives, so to speak, the phases of His own existence:

> I am the first and the last, and alive, and was dead and behold I am living for ever and ever, and have the keys of death and hell (REV 1:17-18).

Yet there is no more undivided, no more simplified existence than the existence of the Son of God, as He exists through the unchanging duration of the Word. The successive phases He describes are yet one life. So for the Christian life and death are one life, through the unchanging oneness of Christ's personality. "Therefore whether we live, or whether we die, we are the Lord's" (ROM 14:8).

Our Christian Minds then find, in the grace of Christ's total proprietorship over us, that wonderful philosophy which has been man's dream from the beginning, but which has proved a mere illusion outside the grace of the Incarnation, I mean a practical and workable conviction that life and death, at bottom, are one and the same thing.

The preceding considerations may serve as a commentary on another passage in St. Paul's Epistles, as beautiful and significant as the one in the letter to the Romans. It is in the Epistle to the Philippians, and I need hardly do more than just quote it:

> According to my expectation and hope: that in nothing I shall be confounded, but with all confidence, as always, so now also shall Christ be magnified in my body, whether it be by life or by death. For to me, to live is Christ: and to die is gain. And if to live in the flesh, this is to me the fruit of labor, and what I shall choose I know not. But I am straitened between two: having a desire to be dissolved and to be with Christ, a thing by far the better. But to abide still in the flesh is needful for you. And having this confidence, I

know that I shall abide and continue with you all, for your furtherance and joy of faith (Phil 1:20-25).

The occasion for Paul to pour out his innermost feeling in the manner he does here is different from the circumstance that brought about that great mental flight of his when writing to the Romans. With the Philippians it is the anticipation of a possible separation from his dear friends through death. But the leading idea is the same: death or no death, it is all one in Christ. Life is profitableness in Christ, death is nearerness unto Christ. It is difficult to choose between two such excellent states: "And what to choose, I know not" (Phil 1:22).

A third passage with the same ultimate meaning is to be found in the second Epistle to the Corinthians. Life is there described as a bodily absence from the Lord, whilst death, which implies an absence from the body, results in a presence with the Lord. But the practical mental attitude is the same for life and death:

And therefore we labour, whether absent or present, to please him (2 Cor 5:9).

The frightful hiatus between life and death is one of the things that seem most repulsive to the modern mind. The modern mind wants continuity in all things. One of the commonest efforts to suppress the hiatus, is the exhortation to feel happy at the thought that man's personality at death passes into the great Universe as a new force.

In order to preserve continuity of life, men sacrifice personality. Yet man will not go to Christ for the very thing he yearns for:

And you will not come to me that you may have life (John 5:40).

As a philosophy the continuance is of course a deeper concept than the hiatus. But it is only the Christian Mind that reconciles continuance of life with continuance of personality.

XIV
THE ATTITUDE OF THE CHRISTIAN MIND TOWARDS THEM THAT FALL ASLEEP IN THE LORD

The Catholic doctrine implied in the rather vague term "Purgatory" is certainly the one tenet of our holy faith where man's imaginations have the greatest chance of crowding out the solid and definite facts of ecclesiastical teaching.

There is the constant danger with pious people of giving too great a preponderance to what I might call the spiritistic side of this doctrine, with a tendency of laying too much stress on the state of disembodiment of the human soul, a state which results in new conditions of existence for the faithful departed of a mysterious and painful nature. The predominant idea, however, that ought to shape our whole mental outlook in this matter is the great fact that death for the Christian is essentially a falling asleep in the Lord.

No greater error could be committed than to suppose that the Christian soul from the moment of its baptismal regeneration up to the moment of being introduced to the Blessed Vision of God in Heaven is ever to pass through a phase of existence where its membership with Christ would be less accentuated, or almost suspended. This vital force of membership with the living Son of God is the one certain spiritual fact in the history of the Christian's soul about which there can be no doubts, and all other doctrines are, so to speak, essentially subservient to that dominating factor.

To assert that in the state of the disembodiment of the soul conveyed by the term "Purgatory" the life of redeemed man is less entirely a life in Christ than it is here on earth, would be a statement as gratuitous as it is dangerous. Nowhere in the Scriptures, nowhere in theology or tradition is there any trace of such a diminution of the soul's membership with Christ. On the contrary, everywhere we find that the life of man in Christ and Christ's life in man are, from their very nature, not only continuous, but perfectly progressive.

Mortal sin is the only thing that interferes substantially with the flow of the great life. It is far from my purpose to write a treatise on Purgatory. I am concerned here exclusively with the mental attitude of the Catholic, with the question how we ought to view practically the state of the Christian soul departed from the body, and not yet admitted to the fullness of God's vision because personal sin is not fully expiated.

First of all there is nothing in the Catholic doctrine on Purgatory that could make it inappropriate to apply to every dead Christian the beautiful expression that "he fell asleep in the Lord," if he died in the faith of the Son of God, and if there are the ordinary indications that he passed out of this world in the state of grace. Though it may be presumed, according to Catholic sentiment, that many who die in the charity of Christ, have still to atone, are still slightly tarnished in beauty of soul, yet such a fear, whatever its foundations and its nature, ought in no wise to render us less eager to use the dear old phrase with regard to our departed fellow Christians: They are asleep in the Lord, all of them.

The language of the Apostolic age and the words of the liturgy of the Church in all times are quite unhesitating in this matter. Everywhere the dying Christian is represented as falling asleep in the Lord, and there are no other terrors for him than the evil of being separated from the Lord and thus falling a prey to the dragon. The suffering of Purgatory. is not one of the terrors of the dying Christian.

To die in the peace of Christ, *in osculo Domini,* with the "kiss" from the Lord's lips on the soul's innermost consciousness, is the one overpowering fact. Whatever happens to the Christian soul after its departure from the body is governed by that great fact of Christ's friendship with the saved spirit.

It is of course one of the apparent anomalies of Catholic doctrine that there should be atonement or suffering of spirit for the disembodied Christian soul, on the one hand, and the peace of immutable life in Christ, on the other hand, in that mysterious state of cleansing. Yet our knowledge as to the nature of that cleansing is very limited. We know that it exists in the case of many of the faithful departed. But we know a vast deal more as to the condition of man's incorporation in Christ.

If we open the Scriptures, this great spiritual reality is the one doctrine that has been worked out by the sacred writers with greatest completeness. The soul's destiny is forever modified by that wonderful incorporation in Christ's living organism. To view the soul's state outside it would be a most dangerous mental attitude.

A Purgatory that is not life in Christ has nothing to do with Catholic dogma. For cautious as the Church is with regard to the nature of the cleansing process, its duration, its extent, the exhortation to pray for the departed is constantly on the lips of Holy Mother the Church. In practice it is the only view of Purgatory that appeals to the Church, that makes the Church class it amongst her life-giving doctrines. She wants the faithful here on earth to realize that in virtue of the great incorporation in Christ we all, living and dead, can contribute towards the increase of the divine life, and through our own sanctity here on earth, our prayers, our charity, our good works, we have it in our power to bring the divine life of the departed Christian soul to its full development of joy and glory.

As to what I called a moment ago the spiritistic side of Purgatory, the state of the soul in Purgatory, the Church never professed to hold any explicit revelation. Purgatory is to her essentially part of the mystery of the Incarnation; it is the body of Christ, with its variety of functions and affections.

One of the scriptural utterances of which Catholic theologians make use in order to establish dogmatically the existence of a purifying process for certain souls, though the souls be founded in grace, is from the first Epistle to the Corinthians.

> According to the grace of God that is given to me, as a wise architect I have laid the foundation: and another buildeth thereon. But let every man take heed how he buildeth thereupon. For other foundation no man can lay, but that which is laid which is Christ Jesus. Now, if any man build upon this foundation gold, silver, precious stones, wood, hay, stubble, every man's work shall be manifest; for the day of the Lord shall declare it, because it shall be revealed in fire; and the fire shall try every man's work, of what sort it is. If any man's work abide, which he hath built thereupon, he shall receive a reward. If any man's work burn, he shall suffer loss; but he himself shall be saved, yet so as by fire. Know you not that you are the temple of God, and that the Spirit of God dwelleth in you (1 Cor 3:10-16)?

The main idea of St. Paul is very clear. He admits that the teachers of the New Testament may be found to do bad work on a very good foundation, Christ. Yet it is not such bad work as to be a cause of eternal loss. On the other hand, the judgment of Christ will be as keen as fire. It will burn the bad work, but will leave the foundation, Christ. It is essentially a rectifying of an imperfection, not a destruction of a sinner.

The metaphors then of St. Paul convey a clear spiritual principle, the principle that God's judgments act as fire even on the just. And as the expression "the day of the Lord" implies a judgment that is beyond the present state of mortality, theologians are justified in seeing here a general principle of which Purgatory is one of the applications.

I need not tarry in showing how far it is legitimate for the theologian to deduce from the above text the doctrine of a purifying process for departed Christians. The inference is fully justified. But my concern is with the broader issue stated by St. Paul, that through all the fire and loss, there is one thing that remains unmoved and untouched, the foundation that was laid, Christ Himself. "For other foundation no man can lay, but that which is laid, which is Christ Jesus" (1 COR 3:11).

My conclusion then is that the one classical text in favor of the purifying process for souls lays the greatest stress on the permanency of Christ's abiding presence through all the imperfections of spiritual work, and the subsequent trial by fire. More than any other province of reality, this great reality, the state of the disembodied Christian soul, is to be approached through Christ, and in Christ. If we walk into it regardless of the grace of the Incarnation that broods over it all, we turn a mystery of mercy into a vague shadow of horror.

In strict dogmatic language there are three states of existence for the Christian. First there is the state of mortality, here on earth, with its struggles and sufferings. It is for the Christian essentially a knowledge of, and participation in, Christ's sufferings. Then there is the state of glory, which is indissolubly combined with the resurrection of the body, as an outcome of Christ's resurrection. It is the true *Ecclesia triumphans* (Church Triumphant).

Between those two states, there is the transient, accidental, and less universal state of those that fell asleep in the Lord, a state that means happiness and gain, as according to the language of St. Paul it is better to be absent from the body, and to be present to the Lord.

> But we are confident, and have a good will to be absent rather from the body, and to be present with the Lord (2 COR 5:8).

This intermediary state is less clearly described to us than the two other states. Its psychological conditions are a mystery to us. It caused the first practical perplexity to the early Christians, the converts of the Apostles. The Apostolic preaching was all about the great triumph of Christ coming in glory, with the concomitant glorification of the elect, completely transformed in soul and body. But when the number of those Christians who died before the great manifestation of Christ increased in the churches, the question began to be asked what became of them, what hopes they had of seeing Christ on the day of His power. St. Paul answers the difficulty in his first Epistle to the Thessalonians, fourth chapter:

> And we will not have you ignorant, brethren, concerning them that are asleep, that you be not sorrowful, even as others who have no hope. For if we believe that Jesus died and rose again: even so them who have slept through Jesus will God bring with him. For this we say unto you in the word of the Lord, that we who are alive, who remain unto the coming of the Lord, shall not prevent them who have slept. For the Lord Himself shall come down from Heaven with commandment, and with the voice of an Archangel, and with the trumpet of God: and the dead who are in Christ shall rise first. Then we who are alive, who are left, shall be taken up together with them in the clouds to meet Christ, into the air, and so shall we be always with the Lord. Wherefore comfort ye one another with these words (1 Thess 4:12-17).

Yet with all that consoling message as to the share the dead Christian will have one day in Christ's resurrection, the Apostle refrains from saying anything concerning the life of those souls in their present state of disembodiment. With St. Paul, the mystery of the resurrection is, so to speak, the only thing that matters. What is of importance, is to establish the fact that God will give the dead Christian the full privilege of the final resurrection.

Whatever may be the intermediate mode of life for the soul, all due guarantee as to its happiness is given us through the assertion that such a state, as all other concerns of the baptized soul, is a thing in the Lord. In the Epistle to the Philippians St. Paul declares most emphatically that death means life with the Lord:

> But I am straitened between two: having a desire to be dissolved and to be with Christ, a thing by far the better. But to abide still in the flesh, is needful for you (Phil 1:23-24).

No more satisfactory formula could be found for our own minds in which to express the state and conditions of life of the faithful departed, of whatever rank of sanctity they may be, than the old expression "asleep in the Lord."

The subdivision of this middle state into souls perfect in bliss, and souls in need of prayer and suffrages is, I might almost say, a minor distinction. It does not bring about distinct kinds of existence. We might call it two unequal conditions inside the same state of existence. And it is my conviction that a very great service would be rendered to the Christian Mind if it could be brought to think of all departed Christian souls in that truly divinized fashion.

Our concern with the spirits of the just departed is a practical one, praying for them, or even praying to them. Both these functions of spiritual life are unthinkable unless they be part of our life in Christ. It is true that in common Catholic parlance the Church is divided into *Ecclesia militans* (Church Militant), *Ecclesia patiens* (Church Suffering), and *Ecclesia triumphans* (Church Triumphant), which division comprises the Christian here on earth fighting the battles of God, the souls in Purgatory atoning for the negligences of life, and the assembly of the saved souls in the bliss of Heaven.

Such a division is quite legitimate, as it is concerned not so much with different kinds of existence, as with different conditions of happiness. The older division however gives greater satisfaction to the intellect. It means three totally different states of existence, mortal life, the disembodied life, and the risen life of, the Christian.

The more modern division has reference chiefly to the order of things that obtains at present, leaving out of sight that totally new mode of existence that will come to man on the day when he will rise in his flesh endowed with incorruption.

If pressed too much, the modern division might create the impression that there is as real a difference in the mode of existence between the soul that is still kept from the clear Vision of God, and the soul admitted to that Vision, as there is between the struggling Christian here on earth, still exposed to all the perils of the trial, and the disembodied soul of the Christian, who passed out of this world in the charity of Christ. Yet it is evident the two differences have nothing in common. The soul in Purgatory is forever established in grace; sin has become quite impossible.

The Church in her official capacity pronounces on the sanctity of a Christian's earthly life; she has the right to declare that the soul is in the glory of Heaven. But at no time could the Church pronounce in an individual case whether or not a soul passes, or has passed, through the cleansing fire. The possible delays that keep the saved soul from the full enjoyment of beatific bliss do not really constitute an essentially different state, as all souls that are saved live in Christ unto God.

I feel sure that the reader will pardon this insistence on a view which today perhaps is getting less common. Yet if anything is precious to the Christian Mind, it is the consideration that life in Christ is one continuous, uninterrupted flow, from baptism on till the glorious resurrection of the last day.

XV

CHRIST THE JUDGE OF THE LIVING AND THE DEAD

The role of judge has been attributed to God at all stages of religious faith. Not only does man expect fair dealing for himself on the part of God, but he considers Divinity as holding the office of judge over mankind, rewarding the good, punishing the wicked, and redressing the balance of good and evil in His own good time. The idea pervades the writings of the Old Testament:

> Far be it from thee to do this thing and to slay the just with the wicked, and for the just to be in like case as the wicked, this is not beseeming thee: thou who judgest all the earth will not make this judgment (GEN 18:25).

Thus spoke Abraham to Jehovah, as he walked with the Lord on the way to Sodom, and as he prayed that the guilty city might be spared for the sake of fifty just men if perchance such a number could be found there.

> The just shall rejoice when he shall see revenge: he shall wash his hands in the blood of the sinner. And man shall say: If indeed there be fruit to the just: there is indeed a God that judgeth them on the earth (Ps 57:11-12).

Belief in the great day of judgment at the end of the world is one of the most constant themes of inspiration for the teachers and seers of Israel:

> Then shall the just stand with great constancy against those that have afflicted them, and taken away their labors (Wis 5:1).

The whole of the fifth chapter of the Book of Wisdom could be quoted as an illustration of the Jewish belief in the great final judgment with its glories and its horrors. As for the prophets, one might fill a book with their utterances about the judgment to come.

> Wherefore expect me, saith the Lord, in the day of my resurrection that is to come, for my judgment is to assemble the Gentiles, and together the kingdoms: and to pour upon them my indignation and all my fierce anger: for with the fire of my jealousy shall all the earth be devoured (Zeph 3:8).

No doubt "the day of darkness and of gloominess, the day of clouds and whirlwinds" (Joel 2:2), in the mind of the seer is not always the last day of the world: it is some definite time in which God gathers up the crimes of men as in a bundle, and throws them into the furnace of His anger, without bringing mankind as a whole to His bar. Yet the idea of a universal retribution and settlement of accounts at the end of mankind's history is so forcibly stated by the prophets that the point needs no further elaboration here.

The concept then of God as the great Judge, and also the concept of the universal judgment at the end of the world, could in no wise be called a specifically Christian concept, flowing from the central doctrine of the Incarnation. Christ found the doctrine well established, and He lent it the weight of His authority. The end of the world with its concomitant judgment was an idea familiar to the people that thronged to hear Him. He gave it greater splendor and luminousness through the clearness of His statements, and the definiteness of the parables in which He embodied the teaching.

The parable of the wheat and cockle, where "the harvest is the end of the world and the reapers are the Angels" (Matt 13:39), presupposes in the minds of the listeners a high degree of faith in the Last Day, besides its being a statement of the great truth in words of matchless effectiveness.

Even therefore as cockle is gathered up and burnt with fire: so shall it be at the end of the world (Matt 13:40).

Yet in this matter of God's role as judge Christ has done something more than throw additional light and brilliancy on a subject already believed in. Though the doctrine in its broader terms is not specifically an outcome of the Incarnation, our Lord appropriated it in a way He has not followed in other matters.

He Himself is the great central figure of that doctrine, He Himself is the judge, the judgment Day will be essentially His own Day. He will come in glory with the Angels, and mankind will be brought to Him. His followers and friends will sit with Him, as His assessors, and the dividing between the good and the wicked will be done entirely on Incarnation lines, if I may use the expression.

The good are those that gave Him to eat when He was hungry, gave Him to drink when He was thirsty, visited Him when He was in prison. The wicked owe their reprobation to the neglect of those offices towards Him. For St. Paul as well as for the other writers of the New Testament, the great day spoken of by the prophets of old has a new significance, not only a new splendor.

It is the day of the Lord. The world's condemnation is merely part of it. The great fact of that day is the triumphant manifestation of Christ.

I am thus justified, I think, in placing the doctrine of the judgment amongst the specifically Christian doctrines, because it is so inseparably united with Christ's person, so completely identified with Him, that the doctrine, and the idea of judgment such as we find it at the end of the Old Testament, differs as much from the concept of Judgment at the end of the New Testament as the graces of the ordinary Providence differ from the graces of the Incarnation. Here we have more than an elevation of a preexisting idea; we have a complete transformation of it.

Judgment will be done as was the belief of Patriarchs and Prophets, but it will be judgment by a "man", as St. Paul puts it in his discourse to the Areopagus:

> And God indeed having winked at the times of this ignorance, now declareth unto men that all should everywhere do penance. Because he hath appointed a day wherein he will judge the world in equity by the man whom he hath appointed; giving faith to all by raising him up from the dead (ACTS 17:30-31).

This transference of the divine judicial function to the Son of God *qua* man, is solemnly announced by Christ Himself. For "neither doth the Father judge any man: but hath given all judgment to the Son" (JOHN 5:22). It belongs properly to a dogmatic treaty on the Incarnation to explain this handing over to the Son of the function of judge. It is part of the mystery of the elevation of Christ's human nature through the Hypostatic Union, as explained in the third chapter of this book. But without any deeper investigations into that glorious truth of Christ's exaltation *qua* man, such words as are here quoted ought to suffice to establish the contention thus put forward, that the general doctrine of God's judicial power has been profoundly modified and affected by the Incarnation.

The deepest modification of the preexisting belief is of course the fact that it will be Christ in the glory of His manhood who will execute all judgment. It will be His mighty voice as man, that will open up the graves, and call all generations to His judgment seat:

> Amen, amen, I say unto you that the hour cometh, and now is, when the dead shall hear the voice of the Son of God, and they that hear shall live. For as the Father hath life in himself, so he hath given to the Son also to have life in himself: And he hath given him power to do judgment, because he is the Son of man. Wonder not

at this: for the hour cometh, wherein all that are in the graves shall hear the voice of the Son of God (JOHN 5:25-28).

But there is more than this wonderful handing over to Christ of the divine prerogative. The great judgment at the end of time is essentially a justification and glorification of Christ, Who has been the most reviled and the most ill-treated of all that ever lived on this earth. Such is Christ's own bold confession at the moment of His greatest humiliation, when He stood as a captured malefactor before the high-priest:

> And the high-priest rising up, said to him: Answerest thou nothing to the things which these witness against thee? But Jesus held his peace. And the high priest said to him: I adjure thee by the living God, that thou tell us if thou be the Christ, the Son of God. Jesus saith to him: Thou hast said it. Nevertheless I say to you, hereafter you shall see the Son of man sitting on the right hand of the power of God, and coming in the clouds of heaven. Then the high priest rent his garments, saying: he hath blasphemed, what further need have we of witnesses? Behold, now you have heard the blasphemy: What think you? But they answering said: he is guilty of death (MATT 26:62-66).

His apparition in the glory of a judge will raise an immense wail in mankind, a wail of regret and despair, because they have so obstinately discarded Him:

> Behold, he cometh with the clouds, and every eye shall see him, and they also that pierced him. And all the tribes of the earth shall bewail themselves because of him. Even so. Amen (REV 1:7).

In the second place, mankind will be judged in reference to Christ's presence here on earth, either in His own Person, or in the person of His followers. My reader will easily forgive me if I quote the whole passage from St. Matthew's Gospel, where the Son of God declares so emphatically that personal element in His judgment to come, praising and condemning mankind according to their attitude towards Himself in His human needs:

> And when the Son of man shall come in his majesty, and all the Angels with him, then shall he sit upon the seat of his majesty. And all nations shall be gathered together before him, and he shall separate them one from another, as the shepherd separateth the sheep from the goats: And he shall set the sheep on his right hand, but the goats on his left. Then shall the king say to them that shall be on his right hand: Come, ye blessed of my Father, possess you the kingdom prepared for you from the foundation of the world. For I was hungry, and you gave me to eat: I was thirsty, and you gave me to drink: I was a stranger and you took me in: naked, and you covered me, sick and you visited me: I was in prison and you came to me. Then shall the just answer him, saying: Lord, when did we see thee hungry, and fed thee: thirsty, and gave thee drink? And when did we see thee a stranger, and took thee in? or naked and covered thee? Or when did we see thee sick or in prison, and came to thee? And the king answering, shall say to them: Amen I say to you, as long as you did it to one of these my least brethren, you did it to me. Then he shall say to them also that shall be on his left hand: Depart from me, you cursed, into everlasting fire, which was prepared for the devil and his angels. For I was hungry, and you gave me not to eat: I was thirsty, and you gave me not to drink. I was a stranger, and you took me not in: naked, and you covered me not: sick, and in prison, and you did not visit me. Then they also shall answer him, saying: Lord, when did we see thee hungry, or thirsty, or a stranger, or naked, or sick, or in prison, and did not minister to thee? Then he shall answer them, saying: Amen I say to you, as long as you did it not for one of these least, neither did you do it to me. And these shall go into everlasting punishment: but the just, into life everlasting (MATT 25:31-46).

It could hardly be asserted with any degree of accuracy that Christ speaks of the judgment of such people only as knew His law and Gospel, and not of the generality of men. The words of the Gospel are as comprehensive and general as they could possibly be. Every human creature seems to be included in the great tableau.

St. Paul, in the second chapter of the Epistle to the Romans, speaks expressly of God's judgments over Jew and Gentile irrespective of the actual and positive knowledge of the Gospel. Yet he too makes of the judgment of such people a thing intimately connected with Christ and His Gospel:

> For when the Gentiles who have not the law, do by nature those things that are of the law; these having not the law, are a law to themselves: Who show the work of the law written in their hearts, their conscience bearing witness to them and their thoughts between themselves accusing or also defend one another. In the day when God shall judge the secrets of men by Christ Jesus according to my gospel (ROM 2:14-16).

No doubt a more perfect comprehension of the truth of the Incarnation by which God assumed human nature, would remove all intellectual difficulties, and would show to us how justly and fitly mankind's sins against itself are sins against Christ's humanity.

As a third element in the new doctrine of the judgment, such as it is through the Incarnation, I ought to mention Christ's part in destroying the power of Antichrist:

> And then that wicked one shall be revealed, whom the Lord Jesus shall kill with the spirit of his mouth; and shall destroy with the brightness of his coming, him, whose coming is according to the working of Satan, in all power and signs, and lying wonders, and in all seduction of iniquity to them that perish; because they receive not the love of the truth, that they might be saved. Therefore God shall send them the operation of error, to believe lying (2 THESS 2:8-11).

From the preceding passages, and other texts more or less explicit, but all tending towards the same presentment of the end of human history, it is evident that the last great spiritual crisis of mankind will be an almost victorious opposition to the spirit of Christ in its essentials, an opposition embodied in a man, Antichrist, who will succeed temporarily in supplanting Christ's maxims with diametrically opposed maxims. The name Antichrist ought to be taken in its strict significance as an essential and reasoned opposition to Christ in His own characteristic and specific traits.

Now the coming of Christ in the power of judge is not only a destruction of that hater of Christ. but an actual single combat of the two Christs, the true one, and the false one. St. Paul's expression, "whom the Lord Jesus shall kill with the spirit of his mouth", implies more than a destruction of Antichrist's person and empire. It points to a vehemence of action on the part of the Son of God against that wicked man, to which there is no parallel in the Scriptures. The mystery of the last judgment has become, through the Incarnation, a triumphant struggle where the God Incarnate shows His invincible superiority over a fiendish and horrible incarnation of the spirit of error.

There is, lastly, a fourth very profound modification of the universal doctrine of the judgment to be found in the constant promise of Christ, and the constant teaching of the Apostle that Christ's elect will judge the world with Him:

> And Jesus said to them: Amen I say to you, that you, who have followed me, in the regeneration, when the Son of man shall sit on the seat of his majesty, you also shall sit on twelve seats judging the twelve tribes of Israel (MATT 19:28).

St. Paul's sarcastic advice to the Corinthians is a good instance of his practical application not daily life of the glorious philosophy of the Incarnation. They were having paltry litigations before secular judges, but he bids them to make of the mentally unfit among them their arbitrators in temporal matters, since every Christian ought to be fit for the much higher role of judging the world of spirits and men with Christ.

> Dare any of you, having a matter against another, go to be judged before the unjust, and not before the saints? Know you not that the saints shall judge this world? And if the world shall be judged by you, are you unworthy to judge the smallest matters? Know you not that we shall judge angels? how much more the things of this world? If therefore you have judgment of things pertaining to this world, set them to judge, who are the most despised in the church. I speak to your shame. Is it so that there is not among you any one wise man, that is able to judge between his brethren? But brother goeth to law with brother, and that before unbelievers (1 Cor 6:1-6).

This assessorial privilege of the elect is more than a share in the common triumph of Christ and His Gospel. It is part of their mystical union with Him, a union first hidden, as Christ is hidden, then revealed, as Christ is revealed:

> For you are dead: and your life is hid with Christ in God. When Christ shall appear, who is your life; then you also shall appear with him in glory (Col 3:3-4).

The triumph of the saints on the last day was an idea dear to the Jewish mind:

> The just shall shine, and shall run to and fro like sparks among the reeds. They shall judge nations and rule over people, and their Lord shall reign for ever (Wis 3:7-8).

But the personal glorification of Christ Himself, and in His members is a specifically Christian presentment of the last Judgment:

> When he shall come to be glorified in his Saints, and to be made wonderful in all them who have believed: because our testimony was believed upon you in that day (2 Thess 1:10).

I think I have given the leading points that make of the faith in the Judgment an entirely new thing through the Incarnation. It is our duty as Christians to bring our thoughts into conformity with these glorious alterations of a belief, which is as old as the world, and which belongs even to the natural man. Preachers are neglecting their grace in a very grievous way, if they present the judgment day otherwise than as a personal triumph of the Son of God, and His elect.

A keen sense of justice belongs to the Christian, more than to any other man, but it is a thirsting for equity which is personified in Christ, the judge of the living and the dead. The most monstrous injustice, as well as the most cunning falsehood will be brought to light and literally exposed to universal execration by the Son of God:

> Therefore fear them not. For nothing is covered that shall not be revealed: nor hid, that shall not be known (MATT 10:26).

He Himself has suffered so much from the injustice and hypocrisies of man, that we feel intuitively that in Him we have a fellow-sufferer when our sense of justice is offended and exposed like a raw wound to the brutalities of the world. St. Paul shows how we ought to make a practical use of this wonderful outcome of the Incarnation. Misunderstood and misjudged by his own converts, the remembrance of Christ's judicial role enables him to rise superior to that great affliction of mind:

> But to me it is a very small thing to be judged by you, or by man's day: but neither do I judge my own self. For I am not conscious to myself of anything, yet am I not hereby justified; but he that judgeth me is the Lord. Therefore judge not before the time; until the Lord come, who will bring to light the hidden things of darkness, and will make manifest the counsels of the hearts; and then shall every man have praise from God (1 COR 4:3-6).

XVI

Putting on Christ

In that section of this book which deals with St. Paul's argumentations in favor of the living Christ, as opposed to the dead law, a good deal has been said already concerning the position of the whole ethical order under the Incarnation. But as a clear and firm grasp of this subject is of paramount importance for the formation and cultivation in us of the Christian mind, I intend writing a separate chapter on this very subject. It will be the natural place for the development of many points of view which otherwise could not be brought under one heading.

All up and down St. Paul's letters there are expressions of intense vividness and practicality, all of them deeply original and almost unexpected, so boldly do they cut across our ordinary mode of thinking. They are the voice of the Christian Mind, and though they seem to lack cohesion, they all proceed from the same principle, the identification of Christ with the general ethical order, through the Incarnation.

I am conscious here of one difficulty, a difficulty that haunts me through all my labors in writing this book. It is so difficult to avoid generalities when treating of ethical matters and their transformations through the Incarnation. Ethics are a comprehensive science with classifications and divisions down to the *species specialissima* (most particular type).

Ethics comprise man's moral development in his own subjective self, in his relations with other men, with institutions like the family, the state, and even with mankind as a whole. Even man's duties towards God are part of natural ethics, such as they have been systematized for us by the Greek philosophers.

The Christian school of thought has done little original work in this matter of ethics, as the keen intellects of the Greeks had almost completed the work for all generations to come. Our philosophers and theologians however have done glorious work in systematizing the rules and laws of the supernatural life of grace, and also in working out the harmonies between the natural ethics and the supernatural grace.

But this very completeness of the ethical system, as we possess it now, precludes apparently the possibility of finding in the Apostolic writings statements enough in order to enable us to work out to its last details that transformation of all things ethical in Christ. Thus, for instance, can we expect to find in St. Paul a statement of the virtue of courage in battle which is one of the elements or natural ethics, in terms of the Incarnation, in the manner in which he stated purity in terms of the Incarnation, when he tells us that our bodies are the members of Christ?

It is not my contention, I confess, that we can find the whole ethical order thus restated explicitly by the New Testament writer. Yet something of every class of ethical duties has been thus restated in the New Testament, as occasion arose. And there can be no doubt that the whole ethical order might have been thus restated, down to the *species specialissima* of moral virtues.

Everything that is good and true is good and true in Christ. What has been done explicitly by the Apostolic writers is a guidance to us in those matters which they have had no opportunity to touch upon. Thus, to come back on the example mentioned above, human courage in fighting in a legitimate war, neither St. Paul nor any of the other writers seem to have had opportunities of inculcating it to the disciples of Christ. Yet when one bears in mind how St. Paul treated kindred subjects, such as purity of body and conjugal fidelity, things he states boldly in terms of the Incarnation, one could easily foretell what words he might have used in the other case, had it occurred.

The Christian soldier would have been bidden to be brave in Christ, because Christ also was brave when He fought the powers of evil. It is in this matter of the transformation of the ordinary duties of life in Christ that there is so much scope for our Christian Mind, without any peril of twisting the graces of the Incarnation to purposes that are merely arbitrary.

It is the scope of this chapter to class together and show in their due proportions those casual statements that lift the duties of life from the ethical plane to the plane of the Incarnation, and also to point out further possible applications of the same principle. But there is an important consideration which finds its natural place here, and which is helpful in understanding St. Paul's mental attitude.

It is a well-known psychological phenomenon that man's sense of intimate relationship with Divinity (excuse this rather pagan term) is not necessarily the same thing as a keen moral sense. Many religions full of faith and of the worship or the Divinity are practically severed from all ethical obligations; man is not expected to be true, and pure, and just, because he is religious, and worships God or gods. The old pagan religions were non-ethical, if they were not anti-ethical. A section of the Jewish people in the days of Christ, whilst still keenly religious, were strongly non-ethical.

The same phenomenon has been quite striking at various periods of the history. of Christian nations. But the man who made it into a theological system was Martin Luther. For him a keen sense of man's friendship with God and His Christ was not only compatible both in theory and practice with a non-ethical state of man, but that very friendship was made the excuse for discarding all ethics as superfluous. This is called technically antinomianism, which may be defined as the doctrine that, in the Gospel dispensation, the ethical law is of no obligation.

St. Paul had a double task to fulfill. On the one hand, he had to preach to the world man's freedom in Christ: on the other hand, he had to insist on man's ethical obligations. He makes the two things one by considering all ethical obligations as functions of our life in Christ. His blows from the shoulder on the law of Moses, or rather on its abusive applications, might easily have led to antinomianism; St. Peter signalizes the danger.

> And account the long-suffering of our Lord, salvation; as also our most dear brother Paul, according to the wisdom given him, hath written to you: As also in all his epistles, speaking in them of these things; in which are certain things hard to be understood, which the unlearned and unstable wrest, as they do also the other scriptures, to their own destruction (2 PET 3:15-16).

But St. Paul himself is fully aware of the possible abuse of a most divine privilege. He foresees the tendency of making the liberty in Christ a cloak for malice:

> For you, brethren, have been called unto liberty: only make not liberty an occasion to the flesh, but by charity of the spirit serve one another. For all the law is fulfilled in one word: Thou shalt love thy neighbor as thyself (GAL 5:13-14).

But more powerful than such cautionings are the deeper principles on which St. Paul bases the identity of life in Christ with the whole ethical order. A Christian through his baptism has become so completely one with Christ that moral transgression has become a thing of the past; it is simply incompatible with his new character. If the Christian sins grievously, it is as if Christ died again.

It is this absolute incompatibility between the Christian's spiritual character and transgressions of the moral law which is the central thought of so much that St. Paul writes, chiefly in his epistle to the Romans:

> For in that he died to sin, he died once; but in that he liveth, he liveth unto God: So do you also reckon that you are dead to sin, but alive unto God in Christ Jesus our Lord. Let not sin therefore

reign in your mortal body, so as to obey the lusts thereof. Neither yield ye your members as instruments of iniquity unto sin; but present yourselves to God as those that are alive from the dead, and your members as instruments of justice unto God. For sin shall not have dominion over you; for you are not under the law, but under grace. What then? Shall we sin, because we are not under the law, but under grace? God forbid. Know you not, that to whom you yield yourselves servants to obey, his servants you are whom you obey, whether it be of sin, unto death, or of obedience, unto justice. But thanks be to God, that you were the servants of sin, but have obeyed from the heart, unto that form of doctrine, into which you have been delivered. Being then free from sin we have been made servants of justice (Rom 6:10-18).

Such a doctrine, far from weakening the ethical order, gives it a divine basis, and though it does not give man impeccability, it opens out to him the prospects of a sinlessness that is a participation in Christ's sinlessness. A more complete identification of the ethical order and Christ could not be imagined. That such texts could have been made use of by the German reformer in order to establish his antinominian views, is the most impertinent of all the perversions of the Scriptures.

Where the refined mind of St. Paul sees deep natural incompatibility between the Christian's regenerated soul and sin, the coarse intellect of the German heresiarch sees a complete emancipation from all moral ties.

Far from there being even a vestige of antinomianism in St. Paul's theology, there is in his teaching a distinct belief in a relative sinlessness in the Christian, in virtue of his regeneration in Christ, not the Lutheran sinlessness that comes from man's incapacity of doing any good, a shifting and a denying of all responsibility, but a positive sinlessness made of spiritual strength caused by the abundance of our grace in Christ:

And they that are Christ's have crucified their flesh with the vices and concupiscences (Gal 5:24).

St. Paul speaks of a great spiritual possibility, of a thing accessible to man in virtue of the Incarnation. Rejecting on the one hand a mere system of laws, an ethical order grounded on no life-giving person, the great thinker and Apostle has before his eyes more than an ethical order of a higher rank, more even than an ethical order based on the will of Christ: he contemplates as an ordinary Christian privilege the happy state of such absolute identification with Christ that the breaking of the moral order does not exist practically. Such no doubt was St. Paul's own position and such is the condition of thousands of Christ's chosen ones, at all periods of the Church's history.

Thus this profound principle, so emphatically enunciated by the Apostle, of incompatibility between sin and the regenerate state of the Christian, is the highest elevation and transformation of the ethical order through the Incarnation. With such a principle to start from, the daily tasks of human life ought to assume in our eyes the golden brilliancy of the light of the Hypostatic Union as they did with St. Paul himself, as I shall show now, quoting from many parts of his letters.

The texts have no other logical nexus amongst themselves than the fact of being varied applications of the one and the same fundamental thought. The Christian's duties and attitudes towards his fellow Christian have been expressed by St. Paul in Incarnation terms more frequently and more poignantly than any other forms of moral obligations, as was to be expected.

The noble expression *in visceribus Iesu Chrisi*, "in the bowels of Jesus Christ," is of Pauline origin:

> For God is my witness, how I long after you all in the bowels of Jesus Christ (PHIL 1:8).

To love in the bowels of Christ, is more than to love for the sake of Christ, it is even more than to enter into the sentiments of the Son of God. It is a community of feeling towards the fellow Christian between Paul and Christ so intimate as to be best expressed through the bold metaphor of the identity of the organs of love, a metaphor quite unthinkable outside that supernatural order which is based on the Incarnation. Is there an erotic poet that ever dared to employ such language? Yet with the God Incarnate we feel instinctively that such language is not only permissible, but that it alone expresses adequately a high truth, our love for our fellow Christian. Man's elevation through the Incarnation is to be for ever the pattern to us how to treat, how to receive our brethren:

> Wherefore receive one another, as Christ also hath received you unto the honor of God (ROM 15:7).

Which of us could ever exhaust the practical meaning of such a recommendation, based on such a truth? We are bidden to look on men as Christ has looked on them, and we are to make our elevation in the Incarnation the measure of the honor we pay our brother.

All divisions amongst Christians are condemned for ever by this piercing cry of St. Paul's heart. "*Divisus est Christus?* Is Christ divided" (1 COR 1:13)?

All undue prevalence of merely human considerations, human personalities are made forever ridiculous by that other drastic apostrophe:

> *Numquid Paulus crucifixus est pro vobis, aut in nomine Pauli baptizati estis?* Was Paul then crucified for you? or were you baptized in the name of Paul (1 COR 1:13)?

If Christians understood what they owe to Christ, how totally they belong to Christ, how their whole spiritual glory is Christ's own life in them, they would shun all divisions, all vaingloryings as an insult, nay, as a manual outrage done to Christ.

In virtue of this great appropriation by the Son of God of the individual Christian, the last thing we ought to do is to judge our brother, or to interfere with his legitimate liberties:

> Who art thou that judgeth another man's servant? To his own lord he standeth or falleth. And he shall stand: for God is able to make

him stand. For one judgeth between day and day: and another judgeth every day: let every man abound in his own sense. He that regardeth the day, regardeth it unto the Lord. And he that eateth, eateth to the Lord: for he giveth thanks to God. And he that eateth not, to the Lord eateth not, and giveth thanks to God. For none of us liveth to himself; and no man dieth to himself. For whether we live, we live unto the Lord; or whether we die, we die unto the Lord. Therefore, whether we live, or whether we die, we are the Lord's (Rom 14:4-9).

It is all very glorious doctrine, the highest application of the highest principles of the Incarnation: yet the occasion for propounding it was anything but a deep crisis, it was merely the minor difficulty that had arisen, whether Christians might be allowed to eat the meat that came from the pagan sacrifices and was being retailed in the city shops. St. Paul declares that the Christian is free to do in this matter as he pleases. His liberty is intangible. Yet as a mere precaution of charity, it is better not to eat of that meat, if thereby a weak brother is scandalized, for it is a grievous thing to sadden one for whom Christ died.

> For if, because of thy meat, thy brother be grieved, thou walkest not according to charity. Destroy not him with thy meat, for whom Christ died (Rom 14:15).

> And through thy knowledge shall the weak brother perish, for whom Christ hath died (1 Cor 18:2)?

Look at thy brother, remember that the Son of God died for him. You will be slow to make use even of a right, if by so doing you are in danger of hurting him. After all is not Christ there with His own grand example, not pleasing Himself even in good things?

> Now we that are stronger ought to bear the infirmities of the weak and not to please ourselves. Let every one of you please his neigh-

bor unto good, to edification. For Christ did not please himself, but, as it is written: The reproaches of them that reproached thee, fell upon me (Rom 15:1-3).

But these concessions to the dictates of charity in no wise impair the radical privilege of Christian liberty. Liberty is one of the concepts which can bear being worked out to any extent on Incarnation lines:

> For he that is called in the Lord, being a bondman, is the freeman, of the Lord. Likewise he that is called, being free, is the bondman of Christ. You are bought with a price: be not made the bondslaves of men (Cor 7:22-23).

Even the subjection we owe to our teachers in the faith is no domination over our minds and hearts. In the truest sense, the whole spiritual organization of the Church is for the sake of the governed. Christ alone truly owns us:

> Let no man therefore glory in men. For all things are yours, whether it be Paul, or Apollo, or Cephas, or the world, or life, or death, or things to come, for all are yours; and you are Christ's; and Christ is God's (1 Cor 3:21-23).

That same Christ is man's head and ornament:

> But I would have you know, that the head of every man is Christ; and the head of the woman is the man; and the head of Christ is God (1 Cor 11:3).

Expressions like this, which at first sight seem so casual, for it is a question of behavior at prayer, give us the measure of St. Paul's faith as to the applicability of the Incarnation to every, even the smallest, human problem. There is a question of collecting aims for the poorer brethren. Out comes this high note with its triumphant ring:

> For you know the grace of our Lord Jesus Christ, that being rich he

became poor, for your sakes; that through his poverty you might be rich (2 COR 8:9).

St. Paul defends himself against the charge of unstability of promise and purpose, a grave charge against an Apostle. He thinks at once of Christ, as personifying the stability of God's promises:

Whereas then I was thus minded, did I use lightness? Or, the things that I purpose, do I purpose according to the flesh, that there should be with me It is, and It is not? But God is faithful, for our preaching which was to you, was not It is, and It is not. For the Son of God, Jesus Christ, who was preached among you by us, by me, and Sylvanus, and Timothy, was not, It is, and It is not, but It is, was in him. For all the promises of God are in him, It is; therefore also by him, amen to God, unto our glory (2 COR 1:17-20).

In order to express his successes and failures in the Apostolate he uses the bold metaphor of a smell, the proverbial smell against which one fights in vain. He, Paul is the odor of Christ:

Now thanks be to God, Who always maketh us to triumph in Christ Jesus, and manifesteth the odor of his knowledge by us in every place. For we are the good odor of Christ unto God, in them that are saved, and in them that perish. To the one indeed the odor of death unto death: but to the others the odor of life unto life. And for these things who is so sufficient (2 COR 2:14-17)?

Hospitality is made a divine thing because the guest is received and treated as Christ Himself:

And you know how through infirmity of the flesh I preached the Gospel to you heretofore: and your temptation in my flesh. You despised not, nor rejected: but received me as an angel of God, even as Christ Jesus (GAL 4:13-14).

Gratitude for kindness received counts on the riches of Christ as a repayment:

> But I have all, and abound: I am filled, having received from Epaphroditus the things you sent, an odor of sweetness, an acceptable sacrifice, pleasing to God. And may my God supply all your want, according to his riches in glory in Christ Jesus (Phil 4:18-19).

The relation between master and slave is put on the same lofty and humanizing basis:

> Servants, be obedient to them that are your lords according to the flesh, with fear and trembling, in the simplicity of your heart as to Christ: Not serving to the eye, as it were pleasing men, but, as the servant of Christ doing the will of God from the heart. With a good will serving as to the Lord, and not to men. Knowing that whatsoever good thing any man shall do, the same shall he receive from the Lord, whether he be bond or free (Eph 6:5-10).

The most difficult of all human problems, that of marriage, is enunciated by St. Paul in such language that it is doubtful whether there is any other passage in his letter superior in spiritual beauty to this statement of the most vexed of social questions. Nowhere does the Apostle give us a deeper insight into the meaning of the Incarnation than when he treats of the duties of man and wife:

> Being subject one to another, in the fear of the Lord. Let women be subject to their husbands, as to the Lord: because the husband is the head of the wife: as Christ is the head of the Church. He is the Savior of his body. Therefore as the Church is subject to Christ, so also let the wives be to their husbands in all things. Husbands, love your wives, as Christ also loved the, Church, and delivered himself up for it: that he might sanctify it, cleansing it by the laver of water

in the word of life: that he might present it to himself a glorious Church, not having spot or wrinkle, or any such thing; but that it should be holy, and without blemish. So also ought men to love their wives as their own bodies. He that loveth his wife, loveth himself. For no man ever hated his own flesh but nourisheth and cherisheth it, as also Christ doth the Church (Eph 5:21-29).

Purity and temperance, the most elementary virtues of the reformed man, become in the mind of St. Paul something infinitely more than mere cleanliness of life. They are actually part of that divine cleanliness of Christ's own body. The daring of the Apostle's language makes us easily forget its unsparing directness:

> Meat for the belly, and the belly for the meats; but God shall destroy both it and them: but the body is not for fornication, but for the Lord, and the Lord for the body. Now God hath raised up the Lord, and will raise us up also by his power. Know you not that your bodies are the members of Christ? Shall I then take the members of Christ, and make them the members of an harlot? God forbid. Or know you not, that he who is joined to a harlot, is made one body? For they shall be, saith he, two in one flesh. But he who is joined to the Lord, is one spirit (1 Cor 6:13-17).

It is in connection with cleanliness of life [that] St. Paul uses the beautiful phrase I have taken for the title of this chapter. "Put ye on the Lord Jesus Christ" (Rom 13:14). The Apostle considers the Son of God in the matchless whiteness of His body and soul, and covers himself with it as with a spotless garment:

> Let us walk honestly as in the day: not in rioting and drunkenness, not in chambering and impurities, not in contention and envy: but put ye on the Lord Jesus Christ, and make not provision for the flesh in its concupiscences (Rom 13:13-14).

His own body is forever stamped with the virginity and purity of Christ's body:

> From henceforth let no man be troublesome to me; for I bear the marks of the Lord Jesus in my body (GAL 6:1).

Warning the Ephesians against the rampant lubricities of their pagan surroundings he clinches the matter with this simple phrase, "But you have not so learned Christ" (EPH 4:20).

Unworldliness and other-worldliness become, under St. Paul's pen, most positive spiritual realities. Christ crucified and Christ glorified, are to him unworldliness and other-worldliness, and wherever we may go, nowhere shall we find anything comparable to the matchless powers of expression which the Incarnation mystery gives to St. Paul in order to speak his own contempt of the world. Many a man of genius has tried to say hard things against our vulgar world. But their words are mere human spitefulness. The Christian mind has a triumphant coigne of vantage from which it looks down upon the world, without degrading itself with any sort of spite:

> With Christ I am nailed to the cross. And I live, now not I; but Christ liveth in me. And that I live now in the flesh: I live in the faith of the Son of God, who loved me, and delivered himself for me (GAL 2:19-20).

His courage in battling with his manifold enemies comes from the same source:

> Always bearing about in our body the mortification of Jesus, that the life also of Jesus may be made manifest in our bodies. For we who live are always delivered unto death for Jesus' sake, that the life also of Jesus may be made manifest in our mortal flesh (2 COR 4:10-11).

Men of the stamp of St. Paul keenly feel their usefulness. They know that whilst they have strength and life they are profitable to many. Death to such men is a kind of disappointment, as it puts an end to their activities. But here again the mystery of Christ provides the highest philosophy:

> For God hath not appointed us unto wrath, but unto the purchasing of salvation by our Lord Jesus Christ. Who died for us; that, whether we watch or sleep, we may live together with him. For which cause comfort one another; and edify one another, as you also do (1 Thess 5:9-11).

> For to me, to live is Christ: and to die is gain. And if to live in the flesh, this is to me the fruit of labor, and what I shall choose I know not. But I am straightened between two: having a desire to be dissolved and to be with Christ, a thing by far the better. But to abide still in the flesh is needful for you (Phil 1:21-24).

I consider that this more than philosophical indifference to life and death is one of the choicest traits of the Christian Mind, and it would be ridiculous of any man who is not a believer in the Incarnation to try and copy such an attitude. Activities here on earth are expressed in terms of Christ:

> My little children, of whom I am in labor again, until Christ be formed in you (Gal 4:19).

Our sufferings are sufferings in Christ, our consolations are consolations in Christ:

> For as the sufferings of Christ abound in us, so also by Christ doth our comfort abound (2 Cor 1:5).

But then even when we rest our rest from labor is something divine:

> But we are confident, and have a goodwill to be absent rather from the body, and to be present with the Lord (2 Cor 5:8).

Such then are some of the practical applications of the treasures of the Incarnation to the problems of life and death. The brilliant galaxy of thoughts assembled in this chapter, and coming from all parts of the Pauline letters, have a strictly practical bearing as the reader is fully aware by this time, I feel certain. One thing is clear. We have to inform our lives with the Incarnation not merely by way of imitation, but by taking it as a vital element of activity and courage. We have nothing of our own, "For see your vocation, brethren, that there are not many wise according to the flesh, not many mighty, not many noble" (1 Cor 1:26).

But let no man be disheartened over such destitution. We Christians have an immense advantage to start life with:

> But of him are you in Christ Jesus, who of God is made unto us wisdom, and justice, and redemption (1 Cor 1:30).

XVII
The Christian Mind, The Church, and the Eucharist

I have omitted of set purpose from the preceding chapter several fine passages found in St. Paul's Epistles which at first sight seem to be of the same trend with the inspired phrases I have strung together in a sort of sequence. The texts thus held over have reference more especially to Christ as a power, I might almost say as an executive, amongst the faithful.

Christ is to be trusted and dreaded because He steps in palpably, nay, visibly, into the life of His followers, not merely as a living and life-giving ideal and principle, as a power of grace, but as one who rewards and punishes, helps the well-meaning, and frightens the faithless. It is easy to see how this power of executive adds considerably to the reality of the grace of the Incarnation, and how it gives the Christian mind a very practical, a very positive turn. Nothing could make my meaning clearer than the recitation of those very texts I have purposely held over until now.

The first passage occurs in connection with the excommunication of the incestuous man at Corinth:

> I indeed absent in body, but present in spirit, have already judged, as though I were present, him that hath so done. In the name of our Lord Jesus Christ, you being gathered together and my spirit,

with the power of our Lord Jesus. To deliver such a one to Satan for the destruction of the flesh, that the spirit may be saved in the day of our Lord Jesus Christ (1 Cor 5:3-5).

Then there is the profession of his great powers as an Apostle of Christ in the Second Epistle to the Corinthians.

For the weapons of our warfare are not carnal, but mighty to God unto the pulling down of fortifications, destroying counsels. And every height that exalteth itself against the knowledge of God and bringing into captivity every understanding unto the obedience of Christ; and having in readiness to revenge all disobedience, when your obedience shall be fulfilled. See the things that are according to outward appearance. If any man trust to himself, that he is Christ's, let him think this again with himself, that as he is Christ's, so are we also. For if also I should boast somewhat more of our power, which the Lord hath given us unto edification, and not for your destruction; I should not be ashamed (2 Cor 10:4-9).

Then there is St. Paul's menace to the same Corinthians, in this Epistle, to make them feel the power of Christ, in spite of the apparent weakness of Christ, unless they change their conduct.

Do you seek a proof of Christ that speaketh in me, who towards you is not weak, but is mighty in you? For although he was crucified through weakness, yet he liveth by the power of God. For we also are weak in him: but we shall live with him by the power of God towards you. Try your own selves if you be in the faith; prove ye yourselves. Know you not your own selves, that Christ Jesus is in you, unless perhaps you be reprobates? But I trust that you shall know that we are not reprobates. Now we pray God, that you may do no evil, not that we may appear approved, but you may do that which is good, and that we may be as reprobates (2 Cor 13:3-8).

The first and second passage just quoted are easily understood. The third passage is of a typical Pauline style, and a short commentary will not be amiss. St. Paul evidently was not satisfied with his dear Corinthians:

> Do you seek a proof of Christ that speaketh in me who towards you is not weak, but is mighty in you (2 Cor 13:3)?

Apparently they were under the impression that, in vulgar parlance, his bark was worse than his bite:

> Therefore I write these things being absent, that, being present, I may not deal more severely, according to the power which the Lord hath given me unto edification, and not unto destruction (2 Cor 10:10).

St. Paul gives them a warning. He bids them not to be deceived by the apparent weakness of Christ the crucified and of His poor apostle. For behind that weakness there is the tremendous power of His resurrection. That power Christ means to apply, both immediately, and mediately through His apostle. But there is one condition for the execution of this power. It is put into motion as a chastisement for those only who are Christ's. If a man is not Christ's, if he has been cut away from Christ, the Son of God disdains to show His power towards him. Such a man is a reprobate and the worst thing that could happen to a Christian is this, that he has become such that Christ's power does not reach him anymore, that Christ is powerless towards him. So if the exercise of power with which St. Paul threatens the Corinthians were to remain without its castigating, its visible effects, it would be a terrible revelation of their spiritual state, it would show the fact that they are reprobates.

Then comes that wonderful turn of St. Paul's heart: he is ready to risk his own reputation, to see his power without its effect, to appear a reprobate himself, rather than to see his children suffer from the effects of his excommunication:

> Now we pray God, that you may do no evil, not that we may appear approved, but that you may do that which is good, and that we may be as reprobates (2 COR 10:7).

It is evident that St. Paul had a clear intuition of Christ's executive power in redressing evil amongst the faithful themselves. Christ's power in helping the Apostle and in fact every Christian in the hard struggle against evil is of course part of the general trust in God. Christ is God, and we trust Him to help us:

> Let not your heart be troubled. You believe in God, believe also in me (JOHN 14:1).

It could not be said that practical faith in the power of the Son of God is a specifically Christian thing, except in the sense that we give to the Incarnate Son of God the same confidence as we give the Father. No man knew better than St. Paul how to rely on the power of Christ, in his manifold temptations.

> And he said to me: my grace is sufficient for thee: for power is made perfect in infirmity. Gladly therefore will I glory in infirmities, that the power of Christ may dwell in me. For which cause I please myself in my infirmities, in reproaches, in necessities, in persecutions, in distresses, for Christ. For when I am weak, then am I powerful (2 COR 12:9-10).

But the power of Christ mentioned in the texts quoted above is something more specifically Christian. It is based on the personal relation of the Son of God with the regenerate soul. Its efficacy depends on man's intimacy with Christ, for one that is a "reprobate" will not be attained by that specific power of Jesus. It also differs from the power of judgment, as judgment embraces the good and the bad, the Christian and the infidel, the living and the dead. It is essentially Christ's power over His own mystical body the Church, to keep it pure and healthy.

The act of excommunication on St. Paul's part was only one manifestation, I might almost say, a negative manifestation, of a power that is a most positive, a most life-giving thing, Christ's unceasing energy in building up His own mystical body, the Church.

> For no man ever hated his own flesh; but nourisheth and cherisheth it, as also Christ doth the Church: Because we are members of his body, of his flesh, and of his bones (Eph 5:29-30).

This practical faith in Christ's unceasing activity in His Church to build it up, to purify it, is an integral part of the Christian mind.

I must ask my reader to remember the distinction I made at the beginning of this book between the Christian Mind and Christian dogma. The Christian Mind, in my definition, is the practice, the life-philosophy of the more abstract dogma. Now the dogmatic part of the doctrine of the Church has received great attention in modern times. The heresies, generically known as Protestantism, have forced on Catholics the necessity of stating, and re-stating, with growing emphasis and clearness, the claims of the Church, of the Papacy, of the Hierarchy. It has become the best known portion of our whole theology. But it would be the greatest mistake to think that the aforesaid doctrines are mainly controversial, are mainly a protection against the power of error. The doctrines of the Church of Christ have a most practical side for our individual spiritual life: they make the greatest appeal possible to the Christian mind, because it is there we find the power of Christ applied with unfailing efficacy, nay severity.

Christ is powerful amongst us according to the degree of our faithfulness to Him:

> I am the true vine; and my Father is the husbandman. Every branch in me, that beareth not fruit, he will take away: and every one that beareth fruit, he will purge it, that it may bring forth more fruit (John 15:12).

His great work is the sanctification of the individual souls that are the mystical members of His body; and to that work He brings an infinitude of power, but a power that is something *sui generis*, a power of vitalization and secretion that is a living organism carried to infinite potentiality. It is a power that is both beneficent and unsparing, as all life is. Of this power we have a divinely inspired account in the message delivered by St. John to the seven churches, in the first three chapters of the Apocalypse. There Christ strikes hard in the very souls of His people. His speech is "a sharp two-edged sword" that comes out of His mouth. He kills with death the children of a false prophetess (CHAPTER 2). He vomits out from His mouth the angel of the Church of Laodicea (Chapter 3).

But I must ask my reader to meditate for himself on that most wonderful section of our inspired Books. Then he will see the Son of God in a new role, the role of executive sanctity. It is Christ's role in His Church. The power He exercises is not that power of help on which we trust in all difficulties: it is, I might almost say, immanent in the body of the Church, not external to it. Christ stands "in the midst of the seven golden candlesticks" (REV 1:13):

> He moves them about with a strong arm and He fights against His own careless disciples with the sword of His mouth (REV 2:16).

It is no small part of the Christian Mind to have a keen realization of that work of executive sanctity which the Son of God carries out with unceasing activity and unsurpassable power inside His Church, He Himself being the life that energizes everything and orders everything, and He Himself doing the work of assimilation and secretion.

There is nothing we ought to dread more than the misfortune of putting obstacles to the glorious flow of life in the body of the Church through personal infidelity to grace, or through reluctance in conforming with the mind of the Church. Nothing punishes like stunting a life process, and there is not a life that is more vigorous than Christ in His Church:

I know thy works, that thou art neither cold, nor hot, I would thou wert cold or hot. But because thou art lukewarm, and neither cold nor hot, I will begin to vomit thee out of my mouth (Rev 3:15-16).

Our zeal and fervor to do the works of Christ, if we have the Christian Mind, is more than an ordinary generosity in the service of God. It is a specific love of the life of Christ in us, and in the Church, with its necessary counterpart of fear lest we should at any time put obstacles to that glorious, but unsparing life. We are in dread of the two-edged sword, lest it cut us off like putrid members. As we love the life, so also we dread the life, which is Christ.

Here I find the opportunity of writing down one of St. Paul's most powerful passages, setting forth that absolute reciprocity between our life and Christ's life, a reciprocity founded on the larger mystery of Christ's indwelling power in us and in His Church:

A faithful saying: for if we be dead with him, we shall live also with him. If we suffer, we shall also reign with him. If we deny Him, He will also deny us. If we believe not, He continueth faithful, He cannot deny Himself (2 Tim 2:11-14).

The doctrine of the Church, which Christ builds on Peter, the Rock, is of course a specifically Christian doctrine. It is so intimately connected with the Incarnation that the Church without the Incarnation is not even thinkable. For the Church is essentially and intrinsically the body of Christ, of God Incarnate:

And he hath subjected all things under his feet and hath made him head over all the Church. Which is his body and the fullness of him who is filled all in all (Eph 1:22-23).

But as the Christian Mind takes the practical view of the more abstract dogma, I consider that a realization of the activities of the Son of God inside His Church, activities of mercy and severity, is the practical view corresponding to the great dogma. Our obedience to the Church, our love for her, our devotedness to her, our daring, and our enterprise in her cause, as well as our humble service in the lower grades of usefulness, will spring from such a conviction, as from their natural fountainhead:

> But doing the truth in charity, we may in all things grow up in him who is the head, even Christ: from whom the whole body, being compacted and fitly joined together, by what every joint supplieth, according to the operation in the measure of every part, maketh increase of the body, unto the edifying of itself in charity (Eph 4:15-16).

What I said of the Church applies with equal truth to the doctrine of the Eucharist, which is connected inseparably with the doctrine of the Church. It is a dogma that is of course specifically Christian in tenor. It is as original as the Incarnation itself. It is part of the mystery of the Son of God.

The attitude of the Christian Mind, as something different from the intellectual acceptance of the dogma, and also as something different from the actual partaking of the sacrament, is less easily described on account of the vastness of the object. We may view the Eucharist and make it a most real activity in so many different ways, and the saint is still to be born who has applied to his soul all the treasures which are hidden therein. The Eucharist is the life of Christ, the death of Christ, the resurrection of Christ; it is the companionship of Christ; it is the blessing of Christ, it is the triumph of Christ, as well as His sweet humility.

Our minds see all those things in the Eucharist and many more. He is food and drink, He is priest and victim, He is our introduction to God, and our badge of brotherhood with man in this one and indivisible thing, His Eucharist. It is in the Eucharist that we have a practical demonstration of the vital possibilities of the things of the Incarnation.

The Church does so much with the Eucharist, and who knows what she will do with it in future ages? From time to time a real flash of genius comes over her, and she sees what new use she can make of her great treasure. The modern frequency of the Benediction with the Blessed Sacrament is one of those glorious intuitions concerning the possibilities hidden in her old, old, and infinitely cherished treasure, the mystery of the body and of the blood of Christ.

To St. Paul's mind the dominant feature of the Eucharist mystery is the death of the Lord, shown forth in it:

> For as often as you shall eat this bread and drink the chalice you shall show the death of the Lord, until he come (1 Cor 11:26).

But he sees other spiritual virtues in it. The Eucharist is the sacrament of the union between the faithful:

> The chalice of benediction which we bless, is it not the communion of the blood of Christ? And the bread, is it not the partaking of the body of the Lord? For we, being many, are one bread, one body: all that partake of one bread (1 Cor 10:16-17).

The Eucharist is also the line of division between the Christian and the pagan world as represented by its sacrifices:

> But the things which the heathens sacrifice, they sacrifice to devils and not to God. And I would not that you should be made partakers with devils. You cannot drink the chalice of the Lord and the chalice of devils: you cannot be partakers of the table of the Lord and of the table of devils (1 Cor 10:20-21).

St. Paul has recourse to the Eucharist to decide in a peremptory way what ought to be the Christian's mental attitude with the much mooted question of the meat that came from the heathen sacrifices.

I do not intend to pursue further the possible practical developments of the Christian Mind with regard to the Eucharist, simply because the subject appears to me well-nigh inexhaustible. For all practical purposes the Eucharist is, to the Catholic mind, Christ on earth, with an infinite adaptability to human needs. We need not wonder then if the Church uses the Eucharist as her daily spiritual currency in the Kingdom of God, to purchase grace and salvation for the living and the dead.

Conclusion

On the Sunday after the Epiphany the Church has the following *Introit* for Mass:

> Upon a lofty throne I saw a Man sitting, Whom a multitude of Angels adore singing together: Behold Him the name of Whose empire is "For ever more".

This chant is not taken from any book of the Scriptures, but is a composition of unknown origin. No words could be a more fit finale to this book, whose aim is solely to further the enthronization of the God-Man in the minds of men, as He is enthroned in the intellect of the Angels, and also to foster confidence in the final victory of the ideals of the Christian Mind.

These pages have been written during the great War. One of the chief sorrows of the hour is the realization that even with men who hold the Catholic faith with true loyalty their vaster outlook on things is practically uninfluenced by a directly Christian philosophy of things. Their minds are carried away by merely secular politics; and even then when they practice their religion, as the phrase goes, they are quite devoid of that humility and reserve of judgment which a living faith in the role of Christ as the judge of the living and the dead ought to produce in our minds.

Let them open the book of St. John's Revelation, and they will find there terrifying descriptions of world cataclysms. It matters little what are the special events there prophesied. The gloomiest pen-sketches of St. John are not gloomier than the events of our own days. But what is for our instruction above all things is this, that the seven last plagues, with all the other events described in the Vision, are contained in the Book whose seals the Lamb alone can break.

Whichever way we read the Apocalypse, one thing is in no need of special interpretation: it stands out as clear as the noontide sun. The history of the world is a judgment done by the Son of God. Through all the upheavals of heaven and earth, one scheme is carried through with absolute inerrancy, the Kingdom of Christ:

> And the seventh Angel sounded the trumpet: and there were great voices in heaven, saying: The Kingdom of this word is become our Lord's and his Christ's, and he shall reign for ever and ever (Rev 11:15).

The power of the Son of God, ruling nations and overruling the politics and diplomacies even of upright men, and leading them on to higher purposes, is surely a most direct and most practical derivation of the Incarnation. Yet few even amongst the devout give that power the place in their minds which belongs to it.

They are devout in Christ, but not powerful in Christ. Yet if the Son of God is anything, He is the first and greatest World Power.

In this great and sanguinary debate of men, in which there is no man to lead his fellows to peace, it is the privilege — and an unspeakably great privilege it is — of the Christian Mind, to see "a Man sitting upon a lofty throne, whom a multitude of Angels adore," and the name of that Man is Jesus.

www.ingramcontent.com/pod-product-compliance
Lightning Source LLC
Chambersburg PA
CBHW020006050426
42450CB00005B/335